The Lenin Scenario

This title is one of a series published to commemorate the centenary of V. I. Lenin's death. The others are as follows:

Imperialism and the National Question, V. I. Lenin
The State and Revolution, V. I. Lenin

Lenin's Childhood, Isaac Deutscher
Not by Politics Alone: The Other Lenin, edited by Tamara Deutscher

THE LENIN SCENARIO

Tariq Ali

VERSO
London • New York

First published by Verso 2024
© Tariq Ali 2024

The moral rights of the author have been asserted

1 3 5 7 9 10 8 6 4 2

Verso
UK: 6 Meard Street, London W1F 0EG
US: 388 Atlantic Avenue, Brooklyn, NY 11217
versobooks.com

Verso is the imprint of New Left Books

ISBN-13: 978-1-80429-291-4
ISBN-13: 978-1-80429-293-8 (US EBK)
ISBN-13: 978-1-80429-292-1 (UK EBK)

British Library Cataloguing in Publication Data
A catalogue record for this book is available from the British Library

Library of Congress Cataloging-in-Publication Data

Names: Ali, Tariq, author.
Title: The Lenin scenario / Tariq Ali.
Description: London ; New York : Verso, 2024.
Identifiers: LCCN 2023029715 (print) | LCCN 2023029716 (ebook) |
ISBN
    9781804292914 (paperback) | ISBN 9781804292938 (US ebk) | ISBN
    9781804292921 (UK ebk)
Subjects: LCSH: Lenin, Vladimir Il'ich, 1870–1924 – Drama. | LCGFT:
    Biographical drama. | Drama.
Classification: LCC PR6051.L44 L45 2024 (print) | LCC PR6051.L44
(ebook)
    | DDC 822/.914 – dc23/eng/20230726
LC record available at https://lccn.loc.gov/2023029715
LC ebook record available at https://lccn.loc.gov/2023029716

Typeset in Sabon by Hewer Text UK Ltd, Edinburgh
Printed and bound by CPI Group (UK) Ltd, Croydon, CR0 4YY

CONTENTS

INTRODUCTION

In January 2015, with just over two and a half years left to find a way of marking the centenary of a revolution that shaped the twentieth century, I thought of a movie. Oliver Stone was sceptical but permitted me to write a first draft. One of his two senior producers, Maximilien Arvelaiz, liked it but the big man, he informed me, had underlined two key problems for him, summarised with a Leninist conciseness: 'Too intellectual and too little pussy.' Argument was pointless. Laughter essential.

What about a low-budget movie? Might Ken Loach be interested in a chamber epic? It was not his style at all. Sociology dominates his very fine work, and the lead character in this case was not a worker of either British or Russian extraction. His old script editor, Roger Smith, did like it, and we shared a few glasses discussing various aspects. He wanted more of the Lenin–Martov relationship, but rather than send it on to Godard, via a mutual Palestinian friend, for another rejection, I gave up. Instead, I decided to concentrate on writing a book on Lenin for Verso and burying myself in histories of Russian anarchism, the dominant political current of the nineteenth century. This project did see fruition. A sentence in the introduction read, 'Writing a book on Lenin (given the global intellectual climate) is in itself an act of resistance.' That sentence alone convinced my French fiction publisher, Sabine Wespieser, to publish it in French. Nor did my Spanish and Arab editors let me down, and a surprise Rumanian edition hit the stands in Bucharest.

As for the poor script you are about to read, it languished on the computer, forlorn and forgotten, till one day in October 2016 when I got an invitation from Mark Dornford-May, the artistic director of Isango Ensemble (*Isango* means 'gate' or 'port' in Xhosa and Zulu) from South Africa to come and see their latest production, *A Man of Good Hope*, at the Young Vic. The play is based on a book by Jonny Steinberg, a powerful account of loss and trauma as people flee war in Somalia and economic crises in Zimbabwe and elsewhere in search of refuge in a South Africa which is itself in the grip of global neoliberalism. The clashes between Zimbabwean refugees and unemployed black South Africans were horrific and startling, a phenomenon that could not be explained via racial 'identity politics'. The status of a refugee, regardless of all else, is a universal identity.

The Isango interpretation was truly startling: a lyrical mixture of storytelling and exquisite songs and music. The music directors, Pauline Malefane and Mandisi Dyantyis, are the essential core of every production. Pauline's voice is much loved in her own country but also in other parts of the world where they perform. Apart from new work, they adapted classic operas to local conditions with all-black performers. I watched *The Magic Flute* and *Carmen* on DVD. The latter was particularly striking when performed and filmed against the backdrop of the township in Cape Town, where Isango was set up in 2000.

After the performance, Mark introduced me to Pauline, Mandisi and the rest of their gang, and we drank to more successes. It was while watching the show that a thought occurred to me. Why not explore the possibility of doing an all-black *Lenin*? The present script could serve as the basis for transforming the project into a fully fledged Isango spectacular. How to commemorate it in a way that is both unusual and at the same time has some meaning for a generation that does not even know Lenin's name? A Hollywood-style biopic was clearly not the solution on any level.

What is needed is something that grips the imagination, is austere in both look and budgetary terms. Why not set it in a South African township with an all-black cast and link it to the struggles of that country and its own tormented history? Who could do it? Isango, whose amazing work in setting classical operas in the township have been so imaginative.

I put the idea to Mark, who became excited by the thought. South Africa is one of the few countries where Lenin remains part of the political culture. I sent him the script. He liked it and made notes in the margin on how it could be developed into a very strong, political version in Cape Town. He thought of a classic actor in his fifties who could play Lenin, and it could be done in time for the centenary of the revolution. We had three long sessions in London discussing variants. He could visualise the train, the sealed train making its way across the veld, carrying Lenin and others from Zurich to Petrograd. That was crucial. He could visualise it coming through the veld, entering the township just as workers are putting up a sign: PETROGRAD. We were planning to convey some of the current realities of South Africa while rehearsing and performing *Lenin*.

Two stories. One is African. Hopes betrayed. Illusions sunk. Despair. A few of yesterday's freedom-fighters are multimillionaires, corrupt politicians, and so on. Others carry on, and it is they who decide to continue a project they were working on in clandestinity during the apartheid years that was disrupted by armed police, dogs, arrests and one death. They were rehearsing the seventieth anniversary of the revolution with puppets as part of an illegal school when they were attacked. Some of them now want to mark the centenary to show they are free to do what they wish and that not all the problems have been solved. Mandela was their Lenin? Or was he?

It will be Isango's Lenin, with music and performance, and Lenin will be treated not as a Byzantine saint or a cult figure or villain but as a remarkable human being respected (if hated) by his enemies. And his love for Inessa? How to depict it? They both play the piano, followed by a carefully choreographed dance sequence, a duet exploring the dilemmas. Are love and revolution both impossible? Members of the Isango Ensemble had been told and were very excited about workshopping the new show, and I promised to go and spend two months with the Ensemble in Cape Town. One of the challenges that faced us was bringing to life one of Lenin's shorter texts ('On Ascending a High Mountain') that Brecht, too, had loved but never manage to stage. Mark and I had been thinking about this and imagining various solutions. Should we intersperse the words throughout the play with an image of Lenin climbing as a punctuation mark? Or . . .? The challenge was stimulation.

Let us picture to ourselves a man ascending a very high, steep and hitherto unexplored mountain. Let us assume that he has overcome unprecedented difficulties and dangers and has succeeded in reaching a much higher point than any of his predecessors, but still has not reached the summit. He finds himself in a position where it is not only difficult and dangerous to proceed in the direction and along the path he has chosen, but positively impossible. He is forced to turn back, descend, seek another path, longer, perhaps, but one that will enable him to reach the summit. The descent from the height that no one before him has reached proves, perhaps, to be more dangerous and difficult for our imaginary traveller than the ascent – it is easier to slip; it is not so easy to choose a foothold; there is not that exhilaration that one feels in going upwards, straight to the goal, etc. One has to tie a rope round oneself, spend hours with an alpenstock to cut footholds or a projection to which the rope could be tied firmly; one has to move at a snail's pace, and move downwards, descend, away from the goal; and one does not know where this extremely dangerous and painful descent will end, or whether there is a fairly safe detour by which one can ascend more boldly, more quickly and more directly to the summit.

It would hardly be natural to suppose that a man who had climbed to such an unprecedented height but found himself in such a position did not have his moments of despondency. In all probability these moments would be more numerous, more frequent and harder to bear if he heard the voices of those below, who, through a telescope and from a safe distance, are watching his dangerous descent, which cannot even be described as what the Smena Vekh people call 'ascending with the brakes on'; brakes presuppose a well-designed and tested vehicle, a well-prepared road and previously tested appliances. In this case, however, there is no vehicle, no road, absolutely nothing that had been tested beforehand.

The voices from below ring with malicious joy. They do not conceal it; they chuckle gleefully and shout: 'He'll fall in a minute! Serve him right, the lunatic!' Others try to conceal their malicious Glee ... They moan and raise their eyes to heaven in sorrow, as if to say: 'It grieves us sorely to see our fears justifed! But did not we, who have spent all our lives working out a judicious plan for scaling this mountain, demand that the ascent be postponed until our plan was complete? And if we so vehemently protested against taking this path, which this lunatic is now aban-doning (look, look, he has turned back! He is descending! A single step is taking him hours of preparation! And yet we were roundly abused when time and again we demanded moderation and caution!), if we so fervently censured this lunatic and warned everybody against imitating and help-ing him, we did so entirely because of our devotion to the great plan to scale this mountain, and in order to prevent this great plan from being generally discredited!'

Happily, in the circumstances we have described, our imaginary traveller cannot hear the voices of these people who are 'true friends' of the idea of ascent; if he did, they would probably nauseate him. And nausea, it is said, does not help one to keep a clear head and a firm step, particularly at high altitudes.*

Could we raise the money? To perform it in November 2017 in South Africa and then move it to Europe would not be an easy task but it could be done. The Isango finance experts estimated that mounting the show and filming it would cost just under a million dollars. All this time I had been talking to Z, a Caribbean–American IT multimillionaire. He was a fan of Lenin, Mao and Fidel and had shown the script to some of the better Hollywood types who met me. He had said he liked the idea but could not see it happening. I went back to Z, who, as it happened, funded trade-union organisations in South Africa, and told him the Isango story. He got very excited and said he would fund it. Both Mark and I were convinced it was going to happen and accelerated our planning. I was sent five minutes of a tape: a darkened stage, the chorus building up towards a World War I song: 'The enemy is also at home.'

A day before the contract was due to be signed, Z rang me up: 'I can't do it. It's not you or the play. I don't trust the director.' I was very shocked. It wasn't the money either, but what had happened? Had he been warned off? Why? Mark's credentials, then and now, were more than impeccable. His direction and Pauline's voice are praised the world over. Pulling the plug at the last minute made it very difficult to approach others. Perhaps someone scared him that his trading links with South Africa might be affected. I have no idea. We haven't spoken since.

Tariq Ali
2023

* V. I. Lenin, *Collected Works*, Vol. 33, trans. David Skvirsky and George Hanna, Moscow: Progress Publishers, 1965, pp. 204–5, available at Marxists Internet Archive (marx.org).

Postscript. As I was correcting the proofs of this book, the *New York Times*, followed by others, published a stinging attack on Z and named him. He is Roy Singham and has been accused of being a 'Chinese propagandist' who funds official Beijing views and now lives in Shanghai. The Indian press has joined in the attack because he has funded online mags that denounce Modi and all his works. The absurdity here is that billionaires of every sort fund whomever they want without being attacked by the liberal press. The foolish witch-hunt against Singham is the result of the current cold war unleashed by Washington against China. Anything goes. He should reach out to his Western detractors to point out, 'You'll be pleased to hear that I refused to fund Lenin.'

THE LENIN SCENARIO

St Petersburg, January 1887. Tsarist repression envelops Russia. There is no reform in sight. In this year alone, over 300 pogroms against the Jews were carried out by the Black Hundreds, anti-Semitic squads controlled by the palace.

EXT. CEMETERY – DAY

The city is covered in snow. Several hundred students, men and women, appropriately dressed, marching in silence, have gathered outside the Volkovo Cemetery to commemorate the twenty-fifth anniversary of Dobrolyubov's death. A banner carries his portrait with inscription: OUR DIDEROT. The cemetery gates are sealed. In front of them is a platoon of Cossack soldiers, hands on sabres and whips.

COSSACK OFFICER

The chief of police has ordered there will be no service today. You will return to your dormitories immediately.

Students remain motionless, frozen.

Did you not hear me?

Students suddenly raise fists and burst into song, 'The Marseillaise', and while singing surge forward. The Cossacks wielding whips move and attack. Sabres are drawn. Scuffles. Forty or so students are arrested. The Cossacks charge again, and the students dash in all directions. An isolated Cossack is pulled off his horse, but one of the students steps in to prevent him being badly beaten up: ALEXANDER ULANYOV.

> ALEXANDER
>
> Leave him be. He's little more than a serf. Let's get out of here.

Students scurrying off in many directions to divide their pursuers. Slogans, Cossack curses, etc.

INT/EXT. TINY ROOM. STREET – NIGHT

A week later. A tiny smoke-filled room. Pipes much in evidence. A tiny group of conspirators – two Poles and two Russians, one of whom is Alexander.

> ALEXANDER
>
> I'm still opposed. Before we do this, we must engage in more political activity. I'm not convinced that assassinations work anymore. We have more martyrs on our side and decreasing mass support.

> POLE
> (laughing nervously)
> There will be more political activity than ever *after* we have executed the Tsar. Anyway, we've been talking for hours. Let's do it. Here's the map. Look, this is the route he will take. This is where we will be stationed. Simple. Sasha is unconvinced. We will excuse him, but he has to write the leaflet explaining our actions and appealing for mass uprisings everywhere. Russia, Poland and Finland for a start.

ALEXANDER

Impeccable logic. I am opposed to this, but I must write a justification. OK, OK, I will write it.

POLE

Now! So we can agree on it.

As they walk out of the apartment and disperse, each is followed by Okhrana (secret police) agents waiting outside. Each is picked up in turn.

INT. COURTROOM – DAY

A Russian courtroom. Four students in the dock.

JUDGE

Alexander Ulyanov. The evidence is irrefutable. You were the ringleader in this conspiracy to kill Tsar Alexander III. You do not even bother to deny it. What arrogance in someone so young. Before we pass sentence, have you anything to say?

ALEXANDER

Only this: The monks who insisted that the new Tsar restore the domination of the father over his family, of the landlord over the countryside, and the monarch over all the Russians have signed the death warrant of their Tsar. When it is declared that you can be arrested if you praise the abolition of serfdom, we are left with no other means to act. I accept full responsibility for the decision we took. This Russia you defend is doomed to die. As for me, if I have played a part in helping this process, I have no regrets. Do your worst. I'm prepared.

EXT. PRISON YARD. ST PETERSBURG – DAY. 8 MAY 1887

Beautiful summer's day. Birdsong. Alexander and three fellow students are led into a prison yard and hanged.

EXT. STREET. SIMBIRSK – DAY

Schoolchildren leaving school. YOUNG LENIN *and a schoolmate standing by a wall. Lenin's face is grief-stricken. His friend asks why.*

> YOUNG LENIN
> The Tsar refused my mother's plea for mercy. They have killed Sasha. What use is Latin or music or becoming a lawyer now?

He looks up at the sky, an image of Sasha appears. He runs home with satchel flung over his shoulder ... running to nowhere. His brother's face appears again.

EXT. DAY.

Alexander's funeral. Young Lenin and family follow the hearse.

TITLES

The noise of cannons firing from the Potemkin project the word LENIN, *which fills the screen. Footage from Eisenstein's film as titles proceed. The Odessa Steps sequence as titles end.*

EXT. BAKERY. PARIS – DAY

NADYA *with big basket is shopping, looking very carefully to see what she can afford.*
As Nadya speaks, a set of photographs, a map of Europe showing the cities of exile.

NADYA (VO)

The Japanese victory against Tsarist Russia was the first blow against the autocracy. It triggered the 1905 revolution. Took us all by surprise. It did not last long. Ilyich called it a dress rehearsal. The edifice shook, the building did not fall. Repression multiplied. Many were driven into exile. All Social Democrats were waiting for the curtain to rise again, but the Bolsheviks alone were composing the music.

The conductor with the baton who was rehearsing the orchestra as if they were soldiers on the frontline was Vladimir Ilyich Lenin. I'm biased, of course. He was my companion for over thirty years in prison and exile. We were still in exile twelve years later when a new war erupted.

Archive footage of World War I.

INT. CAFÉ. PARIS.

(VO)

This time the Europeans were fighting each other. The Kaiser against his cousins, against the King and the Tsar, each with lesser allies in tow. The weakest link in the chain broke first. Exhausted, fed-up with the war and starving, the Russian people had had enough. They made a revolution.

EXT. ST PETERSBURG – DAY

TIME FLASH
21–4 February 1917, St Petersburg

NADYA (VO)
Workers pouring out of the Putilov Works march towards the centre of the city. They are chanting 'Down with the war', 'Bread', 'Down with the autocracy.' As they march others, shopworkers, wounded soldiers, and others join them. Soon the squares are occupied. Festive atmosphere. Songs. Speeches being made. Police and Cossacks just watch.

FIRST BYSTANDER
What do they want?

SECOND BYSTANDER
They want bread, peace with the Germans, and equality for the Yids.

FIRST BYSTANDER
Thought as much. Won't be long now. The Cossacks will send them home with bleeding heads.

They walk away. At a distance we see police units putting posters up on the wall asking crowds to disperse. A police

*commander on horseback is reading the message aloud but his
voice is drowned out by angry chants as a large crowd rushes
in his direction. The police withdraw. A hundred yards away a
Cossack unit watches while an* AGITATOR *whips up the crowd.*

AGITATOR

The war has been going on for three bloody years.
Millions of corpses cover the battlefields. Millions of
human beings have been crippled for the rest of their
lives. Europe is like a gigantic human slaughterhouse.

Working men and working women! Mothers and
fathers! Widows and orphans! Wounded and crippled!
We call to all of you who are suffering from the war and
because of the war: Beyond all borders, beyond the reek-
ing battlefields, beyond the devastated cities and villages
– this is the time to get rid of the autocracy. Down with
the Tsar. Down with the war.

For a moment the crowd is stunned then they join in.

AGITATOR

Down with the Tsar. Down with the War.

*A police inspector on horseback at the head of a detachment
attacks the Agitator with his sabre. A Cossack watching
rushes at the inspector and slashes off his hand. The inspector is carried away. The crowd surround the Cossack and
shake his hand, lift him on their shoulders.*

EXT. PALACE

General KHABALOV, *commander of the Petrograd Military
District, and entourage on their way to see the Tsar's ministers. They are greeted outside the palace and taken inside
where they are seated in an anteroom.*

INT. PALACE RECEPTION ROOM

The TSAR *is seated at a desk. His Prime Minister,* TREPOV, *is standing in front of him, head slightly bowed.*

TSAR

Food riots in the city, I hear. Serious?

TREPOV

Nothing we can't sort out, Majesty.

TSAR

Your father, may God rest him, would not have hesitated for a moment.

Flunky enters and whispers to Trepov.

TREPOV

If you will excuse me, Sire, General Khabalov has arrived from the city. With your permission I would like to go and see him.

TSAR

Bring him here.

Exit flunky. As the two men wait, General Khabalov enters, scraping and bowing.

TSAR

Well? Speak up, man.

KHABALOV

Majesty, the situation is under control at the moment. All the squares are occupied, including the Nevsky.

TSAR

They were occupied in 1905, too, if I recall. Your father, Trepov, soon put an end to all that. What was the name of the priest?

TREPOV

Gapon, your majesty.

TSAR
(laughs)
Gapon, Gapon. Yes. What did happen to him? Back to your work, Khabalov. Make sure the garrison is ready. And you, Trepov. Go and settle the matter.

Tsar exits. Khabalov moves closer to Trepov.

KHABALOV

Excellency. The situation is getting worse. The Cossacks are not obeying orders. We might need to divert troops from the front.

TREPOV

The Tsar will not permit that and nor will I. Too dangerous. Where are GUCHKOV and MILIUKOV?

KHABALOV

Watching the show like everyone else. Guchkov's millions cannot stop this any more than we can.

TREPOV

Silence. This is defeatism. If necessary, you will bring out the regiments and clear the squares.

Khabalov bows politely and leaves.

INT. PALACE ROOM

Tsar opens his diary and writes: Nothing much happened today.

INT. 12 SPIEGELGASSE. ZURICH

Lenin's tiny cramped apartment in Zurich. Everything is tidy. Books piled neatly on the kitchen table. He is at his desk writing. KRUPSKAYA *is reading page proofs, making corrections. Loud knocking on the door. She goes to open it.* COBBLER *bursts into the apartment.*

> COBBLER
>
> Where is he? Where is he?

> LENIN
> (standing up)
> I'm here, Herr Kammerer. What's happened? Is all well?

> COBBLER
>
> Is all well? Yes, yes. All is very well. So you haven't seen the papers. There's been a revolution in Russia. Yes, yes, Herr Doctor. It's true.

Lenin and Krupskaya are stunned but try not show it. They look at each other in silence and show the cobbler out thanking him profusely. Then they embrace each other.

> LENIN
>
> Sooner than we thought!

More knocks on the door. A few Russian émigrés are let in. They embrace the couple. One bursts into song. Another opens a bottle.

LENIN

We have to get back. But first let's go and read the
papers.

*They all rush out onto the street, reach the lake where the
newspapers are hanging and read them avidly and intensely.*

LENIN

We have to get back. Convene a meeting of all the exiles.
Nadia, contact Martov. Inessa, cable Shylapnikov in
Stockholm. Tell him to return home now. KAMENEV and
STALIN are in Siberia. They will have to release all the
political prisoners. It's elementary. We have to get back.
I'm fed up with this damned Switzerland.

EXT. STREET. ST PETERSBURG – DAY

*Petersburg. Police are firing on passers-by on the bridge.
Several drop dead. A Cossack unit takes aim at the police
and starts firing. A few policemen fall. The others scatter.
Crowds acclaim the Cossacks.*

INT. CAFÉ. ZURICH – DAY

*Café in Zurich packed with excited Russian emigrants
discussing the latest news.*

LENIN

Enough. How are we going to get back?

MARTOV

We have to appeal to the British and French to let us go
through allied territory.

(laughter)

RADEK

So we can go and agitate against the war? They would love that . . .

MARTOV

What about asking the Germans?

(silence)

LENIN

We might be arrested and shot when we arrive in Petersburg, but otherwise not a bad idea, Juli.

ZINOVIEV

Perhaps we shouldn't go together. Vladimir Ilyich and I could get false Swedish passports and go through Germany.

MARTOV

Do either of you speak Swedish? I thought not.

LENIN

We could pretend to be deaf and dumb.

RADEK

Very bad idea. There is no alternative. We have to ask the Germans. Helphand will be the go-between.

MARTOV/LENIN

No!

RADEK

No other choice. I don't like him either, but he has connections.

MARTOV

If we're going via Germany, we must get permission
from the Executive Committee in Petersburg.

LENIN

Try, by all means. They will never reply.

RADEK

Unless Martov says he's on his own and supports their
policies.

MARTOV

I would never do that.

(everyone laughs)

INT/EXT – NIGHT

*The noise of telegrams being exchanged in the chanceries of
Europe and in Washington, DC.*

British Foreign Office, London

OFFICIAL
(to stenographer)

Cable to Moscow Embassy: Your main priority is to
ensure that Provisional Government remains on side in
the war. Repeat. Main priority.

Quai d'Orsai, Paris

OFFICIAL
(to two stenographers)

A Russian withdrawal from the war is unthinkable.
Inform Prince Lvov that France will not tolerate any

shift from previous position. The war is at a critical stage.

The White House, Washington, DC

PRESIDENT WILSON

You're sure it's a revolution?

SECRETARY OF STATE

There is no doubt.

WILSON

The Tsar?

SECRETARY OF STATE

Our information is that he is about to abdicate.

WILSON

If a bunch of Jewish anarchists seize that country, all hell will freeze over.

SECRETARY OF STATE

Mr President, the argument that we should stand aside and let the Europeans bleed each other is no longer feasible. If the Russian disease spreads to Germany, the whole of Europe could go the same way.

WILSON

Then we must make sure that this doesn't happen. Russia must be quarantined.

SECRETARY OF STATE

At any price?

WILSON

The stakes are high. We have to put all our chips on the table. As a gambling man, you should approve.

SECRETARY OF STATE

Intervention?

WILSON

We have no choice.

INT./EXT. WILHELMSTRASSE. BERLIN – DAY

The Chancery. A well-dressed, self-important man alights from an enormous car and enters the building. He is received by a flunky and taken straight to ZIMMERMAN.

HELPHAND

Herr Zimmerman. You have some news for me?

ZIMMERMAN

Sit down, Helphand. I am for you, but others are not so sure. The Austrian Emperor has written to the Kaiser saying the risk is too great. But the Kaiser is confident of victory, and he says that after we have won, we will crush these Bolsheviks and Mensheviks like flies. Your estimate?

HELPHAND

Of course he will, but let's get them there first so they can stop the war.

ZIMMERMAN

Who else apart from Martov and Lenin? You know these people well from the old days?

HELPHAND

I was very close to Trotsky. Lenin never liked me.
Martov is a lovely human being but can never make up
his mind. Zinoviev is Lenin's right hand.

ZIMMERMAN

Lenin is the key. The only one with a real organisation.
How many of them will travel?

HELPHAND

Thirty or forty. Martov will not leave unless the new
Executive in Petersburg gives them permission. Lenin is
trying to persuade him and is laying down conditions.

ZIMMERMAN

We are supplying the train and *he* is laying down the
conditions. I'm listening.

HELPHAND

It will be a sealed train. Doors will only open in
Stockholm. The train will be given diplomatic status. As
long as they are in it, it will be neutral territory and . . .

ZIMMERMAN
(wearily)

Go away. Get them on the train. Agree to their stupid
demands.

EXT/INT. ST PETERSBURG. BARRACKS – DAY

*Barracks. The Pavlovsky Regiment. Unrest. Soldiers talking
to each other. Officers nervous. The trumpet calls the soldiers
to assemble. They do so, but casually without military preci-
sion. A few have not bothered to put on their trousers. Once
they are assembled, they ignore a command to stand to*

attention. A SOLDIER *walks over to the* OFFICER *and gently takes him away. Another soldier rushes forward.*

SOLDIER

Brothers, we have seen for days what our people are suffering. They starved us on the front while the generals dined on caviar and vodka. They used us like cannon fodder and our wounded are discarded like rubbish. Let us join the working men and women whose suffering is no different. Let us march out and join them. Let us go to the Kresty and release the political prisoners. What do you say, brothers? If we do this, I have no doubt our brothers in the Volhynian and Lithuanian regiments will join us. What say you, brothers?

In response the soldiers roar their approval. Chants of 'Down with the war.' They disarm their frightened officers, removing swords in ritual fashion, breaking them over their knees and then march out onto the streets and fraternise with the workers and others already there.

INT. ST PETERSBURG. GUCHKOV'S MANSION. BALLROOM – EVENING

A bourgeois assembly. Among the generals present – Guchkov, Miliukov. They have been involved in a long discussion and look tired.
   Lackeys come in with vodka. It's served and drunk. Glasses are smashed. Another servant has handed Guchkov a leaflet.

GUCHKOV

One thing will never change. Weddings or funerals. We celebrate them the same. This leaflet is headed 'Down with the Romanov Lackeys'. It refers to us and the officers. Somewhat ironic given what we've just decided.

MILIUKOV

It's the only way. In order to save Holy Russia, we must, regretfully, get rid of the Tsar. He must go.

GENERAL

And what will replace him?

GUCHKOV

To be decided later when the situation is clearer.

MILIUKOV

They've re-established the Soviet.

GUCHKOV

And it is being reported that the German High Command has obliged Lenin with a train. He's on his way back.

GENERAL

Treachery. Treason. He should be hanged the minute he steps on Russian soil.

MILIUKOV

That alone would provoke another revolution, General, and the fires would destroy all of us. A war of manoeuvre, not a frontal assault.

EXT/INT. RAILWAY STATION. ZURICH – DAY

Zurich Station. The sealed train. Only three carriages. The exiles have gathered in numbers to say farewell to the forty who are going. There are children there. At a distance Lenin and Martov go into the station café.

LENIN

Juli, it's foolish to stay here. It was your idea to ask for the train. Come with us. There is much to discuss.

MARTOV

Impossible. They will call us German agents unless we get approval from Petersburg. I have written insisting that unless they approve, we will find other means to return and fight for international socialism.

LENIN

Wake up, Juli. Most of your comrades are desperate to sit in the laps of the bourgeoisie. All the reports suggest that the bourgeoisie, which now has the power, will *not* end this wretched war. Guchkov and Miliukov are no different from Lloyd George and Clemenceau. No different. It's the main demand of the soldiers. This I did not predict. Nor you.

MARTOV

How well I know the way your mind works. Let me guess. We have to make a new revolution that will break with the bourgeoisie, with the men who are negotiating the abdication of the Tsar. That alone will give them more prestige.

LENIN

For how many weeks? Ten? Twelve? We all underestimated the impact of the war. At the conference in Zimmerwald . . .

MARTOV

You said turn the imperialist war into a civil war.

LENIN

Yes, but as a demand. I had no idea that history would make it so concrete so quickly. But it has and so we must abandon the middle stage. From the overthrow of the autocracy, via a miniscule detour, to a socialist republic. Come with us. Let us unite against the common enemy.

MARTOV

Dreaming again?

LENIN

No. Can't you see, Juli? If this is happening in Russia, conditions in Europe, in Germany, France, Italy are even more ripe for socialism. If we can develop and extend the Revolution, it will spread. Join me, Juli! We need you. The others are already backing the war. Tomorrow they will go over en masse to the bourgeoisie. You don't think like them. You know that well.

MARTOV

I do know that, but do I think like you? Comrades Inessa and Grisha are coming to collect you. We will speak soon in Petersburg.

Inessa followed by Zinoviev rush in.

INESSA

He won't come? I told you. The train is getting ready to leave.

Lenin and Martov embrace. All four rush out to the platform.

RADEK

Oh, oh dear, comrade Martov. Missing yet another train.

(laughter. Martov smiles)

MARTOV

With your Austrian passport, Radek, you'll have to wait in Stockholm till Lenin takes power. It might be another twelve years. [To Zinoviev in a whisper:] So the old man is still in love with her.

(Zinoviev smiles and shrugs his shoulders)

ZINOVIEV

At the moment he is only in love with the revolution. And by the way we're going to smuggle Radek in ... He'll be in the baggage compartment.

Both men laugh. Everyone boards the train. Whistles sound. Green flag waved. Train moves off. Lenin looks out of the window sadly and waves to Martov, who does the same. The train pulls away. Martov walks back slowly out of the station in a reverie till he reaches a bench on the lake.

MARTOV (VO)

I should have gone with him. We were so close when the party was united. In Siberia we were like one. On the *Iskra* editorial board as well, until he started with his ultimatums.

It's true that Plekhanov and Zasulich were unreliable. Now they support the war and Lenin feels vindicated. Why did he walk out? I would have backed him. Would I have backed him? Politically I am still close to him, but his style of debate, his political absolutism can be repulsive.

Then he decided to split our great party. Oh, yes, it was him. And why? What was the need? To split on an organisational question! Crazy. I told him that in a rage. Trotsky was in agreement with me.

FLASHBACK. INT. LONDON

TIMEFLASH
1903

MARTOV
We can only win if our movement is united. To split because you favour a party of conspirators, working underground, under a dictator. *You!* Yes, yes, I know the nature of the autocracy. We've all been to Siberia but we're still alive.

LENIN
Only because they don't see us as a threat. Russia is not Germany.

MARTOV
To the outside world it appears as pure madness.

LENIN
Outside world? Ah, yes. When you're watching a man making funny gestures from a distance you think he's mad. When you get closer, you see he's sharpening his axe.

END FLASHBACK

EXT. STREET. ZURICH – DAY

MARTOV (VO)
Now he says, *Look at them, Juli*. Mesmerised by Miliukov's bourgeois rubbish. Your big, wonderful open party in Germany capitulated without shame. Vote for

war credits. Support the war. Can that party remain united with Kautsky wriggling like a water snake and accommodating to the Right and our Rosa in prison?

Everything in Europe will change. He's right. And yet . . . I wish I'd boarded the bloody train. But on the other hand . . .

(Picks up a newspaper and literally jumps for joy)

They've reconvened the Soviet, like in 1905. Where the hell is Trotsky? Could the British really have interned him in Canada? I should have gone with Lenin. Everything is changing so fast. Must write another letter to those incompetents in Petersburg . . .

(Hurries away with determination in his step)

INT/EXT. THE TRAIN

The train. The passengers are excited, tense and nervous as the Swiss scenery floats by. Lenin writing. Zinoviev and Nadya in conversation. Inessa looking at Lenin. As he lifts his head to reflect, he catches her eye. They smile. He carries on writing.

INESSA (VO)

He has the most expressive eyes of anyone I know. I see love in them and softness and passion. Also mockery and a contempt that bites, a thoughtfulness that surprises, an impenetrable coldness and extreme fury. When he laughs, his eyes disappear. I first saw him eight years ago in Paris at a Bolshevik meeting . . . I was thirty-five. He was thirty-nine. They already called him the old man.

FLASHBACK. INT/EXT. PARIS – EARLY EVENING

Paris, 1909, café in the Avenue d'Orleans. Russian émigrés pouring in. Inessa meets a woman friend. Lenin enters, shakes hands. Is introduced rapidly to Inessa. Rushes to the platform.

LENIN

Comrades, today we mark the twenty-eighth anniversary of the Paris Commune. It arose, victoriously from the ruins of the Second Empire and war. After seventy-two epoch-making days, it succumbed heroically under the hail of bullets of the Versailles counterrevolution.

The Commune was, in a far higher sense than the June insurrection of 1848, in Marx's words, the 'most tremendous event in the history of European civil wars' of the nineteenth century. Over 25,000 Communards, men and women and children, were killed by the Versaillaias.

Robespierre and the Jacobins were denounced for sending sixteen hundred aristocrats to the guillotine. Sixteen hundred blue bloods and twenty-five thousand red bloods . . . in this world their blood is always worth more than ours.

(applause)

What we learn from the Commune is this: Never stop halfway. Halt once, and you'll soon be digging your own grave.

(loud applause)

INESSA (VO)

Since French was my mother tongue, I was soon brought into direct contact with him. I would translate, we would go for long walks and bike rides and visit cafés. I fell for him.

Collage of images

He pretended not to notice, but one day we were walking by the river on the Left Bank. It was a summers night. Without any warning, he exploded.

Lenin puts his arm round her waist and kisses her passionately on the lips. Inessa is both startled and delighted. She pulls her head back to laugh and the crease in his eyes expands. He takes her hand and kisses it.

INESSA

You too?

LENIN

Why is that a surprise?

INESSA

They say that your only love is the revolution.

LENIN

They say. They say. Who says?

INESSA

Your close comrades. They say you're a cold-hearted, cruel beast.

Kisses her again with passion. A few bystanders watch them and smile.

INT. PARIS. INESSA'S APARTMENT

Both are lying naked under the covers. He strokes her face tenderly.

> LENIN

What will they say now?

> (She embraces him)

> INESSA

Vladimir Ilyich.

> (He bursts out laughing)

What's the joke?

> LENIN

We're in love, we've made love, and you suddenly address me as if we were at a public meeting and you were about to ask a question. Volodya is fine in private.

> INESSA
> (laughing)

Why not Volchik?

She puts on her dressing gown, runs to the piano and plays Chopin.

> LENIN
> (softly)

Please. Not Chopin. His superficial sentimentality irritates.

She switches to a Beethoven sonata. He puts his hands behind his head and relaxes. While she's playing, she sees him in the mirror above the piano. He creeps out of bed so as not to disturb her, puts on his trousers and shirt and comes and stands behind her, gently stroking her shoulders. She stops playing. They kiss. He sits on the piano stool and plays for her. She's surprised.

LENIN
Do they say all Bolsheviks are uncultivated monsters?

INESSA
No, only that Bolsheviks of Jewish origin can really play music. And Mensheviks are even better. When Martov plays the violin my heart melts.

LENIN
His playing is never self-assured, unlike mine.

He chases her round the room, and she pulls him down on the sofa. They embrace.

END FLASHBACK

INT/EXT. TRAIN

Scenery changes. Train is in Germany and cripples with begging bowls appear as it passes through tiny stations.

INESSA (VO)
It was difficult to conceal our love. He told Nadya. She suggested he leave her and live with me. This he could not bring himself to do. Long years of comradeship and common suffering. We decided to break up, but that didn't work either. Nadya and I talked about it. She said her relationship with him was no longer physical. But she warned. Be careful of his rages, his obsessions. He

can be cruel. The revolution always more important
than any individual.

*She looks at Nadya who nods without smiling. Train pulls
into Frankfurt am Main. Poverty. Thin, weary people with
exhausted eyes moving in a procession past the train. Not a
single smile. Military guard on platform.*
   Swiss liaison with Germans, FRITZ PLATTEN *rushes out to
get some newspapers, coffee, bread, cheese and beer from
the café. He returns with six bedraggled soldiers who board
and hand over the drinks.*

SOLDIER

You are Russian revolutionaries. Yes? All we want now
is peace.

RADEK
(aside)

This country must be collapsing. The beer tastes like
piss.
(to soldiers)
If you want peace, get rid of the leaders who make war.
Start at the top. Once you do, peace will get closer.
Otherwise, it will get worse. The cold, the dark, the
hunger will continue till you are blotted out. German
workers in uniform, you are our brothers. Demand the
release of Rosa Luxemburg . . .

*He embraces them. Others shake hands. Lenin smiles but is
absorbed by a newspaper. An officer enters and orders the
soldiers to leave. Train moves on. Soldiers wave from platform. Radek and others clench fists.*

LENIN
(muttering to himself)
If these reports from Peter are even half-true, the masses
are ahead of the revolution.

INT. THE SOVIET, SMOLNY – DAY.

Petersburg. April 1917. The Soviet is in session.

CHAIRMAN
I agree with the comrade from the barracks. What we
are experiencing is dual power. The Duma determines
the government. The Soviet of Workers' and Soldiers'
Deputies decides what and who goes where.

(applause)

I recognise the Deputy from the railway workers union.

DEPUTY
Railway workers throughout the country have been told
by the union that nothing moves without the permission
of the Soviet. That includes food, weapons and soldiers.
Should we be sending more workers and peasants to die
at the front?

CHAIRMAN
(nervous and worried, whispers to colleague)
Comrade, I understand your motives, but the Soviet is
divided on the war and —

There is some unrest in the chamber.

Order, please. We will discuss this issue tomorrow, and
you will decide.

(applause)

Now before we move on to . . .

INT. MEETING ROOM. SMOLNY – DAY

Office of the Executive Committee ... Members busy answering phones.

> EXEC COM 1
>
> Yes, Soviet of Workers' and Soldiers' Deputies here. Speak up will you!

> VOICE
>
> I'm speaking for the Council of Representatives of the Petersburg Banks. In our opinion considerable order has been restored. Keeping them shut any longer will generate panic.

> EXEC COM 1
>
> What's the attitude of the employees?

> VOICE
>
> All employees are in favour, but we await your permission.

> EXEC COM 1
>
> Very well. Write it up yourselves and send it to Room 13 at the Tauride Palace to be signed and stamped.

> EXEC COM 2/WOMAN
>
> Soviet of Workers' and Soldiers' Deputies.

VOICE 2

Tsarskoye-Selo Railway Station speaking. Commissar, I'm ringing on behalf of the railwaymen. Grand Duke Michael Alexandrovich in Gatchina is asking for a train to go to St Petersburg.

EXEC COM 2/WOMAN
(trying not to laugh)

Inform Citizen Romanov he can go to the station, buy a ticket, and travel in a public train.

VOICE 2

Can I kick his arse if he refuses?

EXEC COM 2/WOMAN

Comrade . . . discipline must be maintained.

VOICE 2

I was only joking Commissar.

The whole room erupts with laughter.

EXT. BERLIN.TRAIN STATION – NIGHT

The sealed train enters Berlin and is transferred to a siding.

INT.

Most are asleep. Radek is snoring. Nadya keeps pushing him a bit to disrupt the snores. Lenin and Inessa playing chess by candlelight. Neither is concentrating on the game. They speak in low voices.

INESSA

Sometimes I wonder if both are impossible.

LENIN

Both?

INESSA

Love and Revolution.

LENIN

Love perhaps, but why revolution? Where do you think
this train is taking us?

INESSA

This one is just beginning. What of those that are over?

LENIN

Meaning?

INESSA

English Revolution. Twenty-six years. Then restoration.

LENIN

French Revolution, if we count Napoleon, twenty-six
years and then restoration and a counter-restoration and
1848 and the Paris Commune. Strong echoes. In
England, too, they had to find a different way to rule.
Revolutions leave their imprint.

INESSA

Russian Revolution? Twenty-six years?

LENIN

Ours is the first planned revolution. Will we succeed in
getting rid of the bourgeoisie. Guchkov and Miliukov

are on the defensive. *They* got the Tsar to abdicate, leaving the structure they support weak and tottering. To succeed, we need Europe. If Germany breaks the chain and a few others follow, the world will be transformed.

INESSA

Hegel might have found it difficult to appreciate your dialectics.

LENIN
(whispers)
And us Bolsheviks. You. Me. We make love and revolution. Impossible?

INESSA

I'll answer when we're back in Russia.
(blows out the candles)

The train's moving again. The train picks up speed.
   As dawn breaks, the excited passengers sight the Baltic. They have reached Sassnitz.

EXT

The Germans accompanying them salute. Lenin ignores them, but Radek can't resist a little harangue.

RADEK

Your tasks are clear. When you return, make a revolution.

PRUSSIAN OFFICER

You are still on German soil.

It's because your troops are still on Russian soil. Soon they will return defeated and demoralised, and what will happen to the Kaiser? Perhaps he and the Tsar could get together and open a hotel in Switzerland.

EXT.

Lenin signals to him, and Radek runs to join them as they board the ferry to Trelleburg. Lenin sighs with relief. Zinoviev joins him. Inessa is looking at the sea from another section of the ferry. She takes a deep breath.

INESSA (VO)

He has to buy some new clothes in Stockholm. He dresses like a tramp. Moth-eaten coats, trousers and socks riddled with holes that Nadya has been mending for years. I will insist. I don't care what she thinks. I don't care what he thinks. It is rare in history for a leader to be able to look ahead, gaze at the horizon and think this century will be ours.

We all have our fantasies. Volchik would never say that, but I know he sometimes dreams it. That's when he's not thinking we'll be arrested as German agents and shot the day we arrive.

INT. ST PETERSBURG. GUCHKOV'S MANSION

Guchkov and Miliukov are alone.

GUCHKOV

Tomorrow? Hmm. Nothing we can do?

MILIUKOV

Lenin is isolated. Some of his Bolsheviks are perfectly happy to move slowly. He won't like that, but nothing he can do. I know what you're thinking. It would be a huge mistake. If we arrest him, we might lose the Soviet before we are ready to strike.

GUCHKOV

And you're sure they will not strike us first?

MILIUKOV

Certain. These are weak people. They can't believe they've got so far. By the way, the British were stupid to arrest Trotsky. I had no option but to ask for his release. He's on his way too.

GUCHKOV

Apart from Lenin, are they all bloody Jews? That will help us. You've spoken to . . .?

MILIUKOV

Yes. The Church will act with us, but please don't be impatient.

INT. SOVIET. SMOLNY. ST PETERSBURG

Executive Committee Office of the Soviet. Worried faces. Chkheidze, *Menshevik* CHAIRMAN *of the Soviet, appears confident.*

CHAIRMAN

There's no dispute. I will officially welcome Lenin back to his country. I hope these exiles have some humility. The revolution happened without them. They should reflect on this fact for a while.

(laughter)

EXT/INT. STOCKHOLM RAILWAY STATION – DAY

Lenin et al. in formal dress are saying farewells. Boarding train. Inside Lenin is reading the Bolshevik paper, his face darkening, his eyes angry. Everyone notices. Nobody says anything.

Train moves on the map to Finland. Another change and it reaches the Russian border. The railway workers at the border station greet the party with cheers.

Kamenev and Stalin board the train and are embraced by Zinoviev, Radel, Krupskaya and others. They walk to where Lenin is seated. He greets them warmly, but then turns on them in a rage.

LENIN

Just been reading *Pravda* under your editorship comrades. Too conciliatory. It's obvious what's going on. The bourgeoisie is going on. Miliukov is planning a coup under your noses, waiting for the Soviet to collapse under the weight of its weaknesses.

That braggart Kerensky is posturing like a bitch on heat, the Mensheviks are behaving as we would expect, and our paper, the voice of our party, is indistinguishable from the others.

KAMENEV

The Soviet is an elected body, Ilyich. It reflects the views of the workers and soldiers —

LENIN

You think I don't know that? I'm unaware of this little detail? How are we going to win the workers over if we have no distinctive position from this, this, this . . . marsh. In such a situation mass consciousness can leap way ahead of the most radical party. We have to be prepared for everything.

(turns to Stalin)

We need to call a meeting of the Central Committee immediately. You were brilliant in organising the bank raids. Now we have to expropriate Guchkov and his gang politically. Central Committee meeting?

STALIN

Of course, but we've got a new headquarters in Petersburg . . . an old palace belonging to one of the Tsar's whores.

INESSA

Her name was Khshesinskaya, and she was a ballerina.

(STALIN smiles at her)

Lenin beckons Zinoviev and Kamenev and the three men are engrossed in talk. Train moves on.

EXT. FINLAND STATION.
ST PETERSBURG – AFTERNOON

A sea of red flags fills the screen. Excited talk and slogans and song. The Finland Station and its surrounds have not witnessed such a large crowd. A huge banner embroidered in gold reads THE CENTRAL COMMITTEE OF THE R.S-D.W.P. (BOLSHEVIKS) is at the head of the credit. Many motors cars. It's getting dark. A huge, mounted search-light is pushed into the square and as it is switched on it illuminates the city, its roofs, its multistorey homes, columns, wires, tramways and human figures. *More and more people are arriving.*

On the platform there is another crowd and soldiers rehearsing their salutes.

BYSTANDER

It's true he will be received in the Tsar's waiting room?

BYSTANDER 2

Who cares? He should ignore the stupid officials and come and talk to us.

INT. FINLAND STATION. TSAR'S WAITING ROOM. ST PETERSBURG – LATE AFTERNOON

The Chairman of the Soviet and five others are waiting. From the windows they can see a large crowd.

EXT. FINLAND STATION. ST PETERSBURG – LATE AFTERNOON/EVENING

Train enters the Finland Station. Immediately the band plays 'The Marseillaise'. The soldiers stiffen, the crowd is expectant. The door opens and Lenin walks out to huge cheers. The soldiers present arms. He receives a huge bouquet of flowers and is hugged. A Bolshevik helps clear the way for Lenin to the Tsar's waiting room. Slowly the room has filled up despite the security.

Lenin enters, his face frozen, emotionless, his eyes cold. Throughout the speech that follows he looks at the ceiling, adjusts his bouquet, looks and smiles at the crowd outside.

CHAIRMAN

Comrade Lenin, in the name of the Petersburg Soviet and the whole revolution, we welcome you to Russia . . .

38

In our opinion the main task is to defend the revolution from within and without. The last thing we require is disunity. We hope you will pursue these goals with us and help to unite all democrats.

Lenin turns his back on the speaker and addresses the rest of the room.

LENIN

Dear comrades, soldiers, sailors and workers! I am happy to greet in your persons the victorious Russian Revolution. I greet you as the vanguard of the world-wide proletarian army.

This war, this piratical war is the beginning of a civil war throughout Europe. The time is not distant when at the call of our comrade Karl Liebknecht the people will turn their arms against their own exploiters. Germany is seething with discontent. The Russian Revolution that you have accomplished has opened a new epoch. Long live the worldwide socialist revolution.

Lenin walks out to the cheering crowd singing 'The Marseillaise'. He goes to the main entrance and is about to enter a closed car, but the crowd will not have it.
There are many soldiers in the crowd. They insist with chants, shouts, hurrahs that he speak to them. Touched, he stands on the bonnet of a car in the square. There is complete silence. The spotlight shines on him and a strip of the crowd.

LENIN

Comrades, I have made it clear to those who came to greet me that we will play no part in this shameful imperialist slaughter that is going on. *No to War!*

(crowd responds by repeating the chant)

All we get from the capitalists and their tame politicians all over Europe are the same lies, the same fraud, different bishops and patriarchs appeal to the same god to bless the slaughter. Enough. We have lost too many workers and peasants fighting for a rotten cause.

With more songs, Lenin is transferred to the top of the armoured car. As the armoured car proceeds, more crowds demand he speaks.

It's a long crawl to the Bolshevik HQ, the Khshesinskaya Palace. A crescendo greets him at the palace. Krupskaya bites her lip. Inessa weeps. Lenin embraces old comrades, veterans from Siberia, others.

As Lenin repeats his words from the balcony, a Soldier gestures from below.

SOLDIER

Ought to stick our bayonets into a fellow like that. Eh? The things he says! Eh? If he came down here, we'd have to show him! And we'd show him alright! Must be a German. Eh, he talks like one.

INT. GUCHKOV'S MANSION.
ST PETERSBURG – NIGHT

Apart from Miliukov, many others are present, including two generals. They look worried.

GUCHKOV

How did this happen? It was huge.

MILIUKOV

The Bolsheviks organise well. Modesty is unknown to them. What is worrying is the number of soldiers present.

GENERAL

Bolshevik agitators came to the barracks and worked them up. Said Lenin was the only leader who could end the war.

GUCHKOV

You couldn't stop them?

GENERAL

No. The situation is too advanced.

GUCHKOV

What would it require to crush this rabble?

GENERAL

We would have to withdraw our crack regiments from the front, and who is to say they wouldn't join the rabble?

MILIUKOV

We have to provoke our enemy into making a false move. Then we make the correct move.

GENERAL

It's not easy to provoke the Germans.

GUCHKOV

He's referring to the Bolsheviks.

MILIUKOV

We need our own agitators. Send in the Black Hundred. Tell them to talk to the soldiers. Lenin is nothing more than a German agent. His party leaders are mainly Jews. Do we want to hand over Holy Russia to Germans and Jews? Look at their new headquarters. Is this how most Russians live?

It's a good start. We need a carefully organised pogrom to destroy the Judeo-Bolshevik conspiracy forever. After that we can decide who should be the new Tsar. Pity the children are mainly girls.

MILIUKOV

And none of the girls are called Catherine.

GENERAL

Gentlemen, the situation on the front is bad. The reality is that our soldiers don't wish to fight anymore. Bolshevik propaganda finds eager ears ...

INT. BOLSHEVIK HQ. ST PETERSBURG – NIGHT

The wooden chairs and tables and the hastily established canteen clash with the opulence of the painted ceilings and the chandeliers. People are going in and out. In the old ball-room there are now chairs and a platform. Seating capacity: 150. The room is filling up with party cadres. In an adjoining room deep in conversation are Lenin and Trotsky surrounded by Zinoviev, Zamenev, Stalin and others. The mood is friendly, even overfriendly.

LENIN

At last. It will strengthen us enormously. Now let's inform the others. Are there journalists present?

STALIN

Yes, but we can get rid of them.

ZINOVIEV

Not necessary ... we need to make this public and stop the rumour factories.

They leave and enter the large meeting room. It's packed with many standing or sitting on the floor. Soon Inessa, Krupskaya, Lenin and Trotsky are sitting on the platform. Others join the audience.

LENIN

Comrades I have a small announcement to make. Comrade Trotsky and all his comrades from the Inter-District Committee have joined our party.

(applause . . . a shout of 'What took them so long?' etc.)

This strengthens our party enormously at a critical time for the revolution.

For many months the press has been referring to Comrade Trotsky and his colleagues as 'non-party Bolsheviks'. Well now they are party Bolsheviks. On our leading committees and the editorial boards of our press. Comrades, our party and our revolution now possess in their ranks the finest pen in the land and the greatest orator of our revolution. Our Danton!

(loud and sustained applause)

Comrade Trotsky has the floor.

TROTSKY

Comrades, we have joined because nothing divides us any longer. We have said rude things about each other, and we can debate who was more vicious in polemic, but that lies in the past. Comrade Lenin's theses on how to move the revolution forward express our views as well. It required courage and audacity to say the war must end and to denounce the conciliatory rubbish that emanates from the leaders of the Soviet. I have no doubt

that we will need a socialist revolution to end this
bloody capitalist war

(loud applause)

*Meeting ends. Trotsky surrounded by well-wishers. A lot of
handshaking, etc.*

INT./EXT.

*A montage of the July Days ... the attempted counterrevolution.
    Lenin fleeing into exile in a wig.
    Bolshevik HQ under attack.
    Bolshevik leaders, Trotsky, Zinoviev, Kamenev arrested.
    Stalin goes underground.
    Lenin writing:*
Now that they have shown their hand, raise the slogan:
ALL POWER TO THE SOVIETS.

EXT. PETER – LATE AFTERNOON

CAPTION
Six months later, October 1917

*St Petersburg. Inessa and Nadya are walking by the river.
Inessa feels Nadya's hands and is horrified. They're freezing.
She puts her own shawl over Nadya's shoulders.*

INESSA
Any news from Finland?

NADYA
Hates the exile but is busy. He's writing a new book on
the state and revolution.

(both women laugh)

44

INESSA

He was right to leave. They would have killed him in July.

NADYA

Without any doubt. That's the head they wanted. But now we really need him back. I fear the comrades are weakening.

INESSA

Even Trotsky?

NADYA

No, not him. He and Ilyich have the same position. Once we are the largest party in the Soviets, we take power.

(she laughs)

INESSA

What?

NADYA

The last letter he sent the Central Committee was so harsh they burnt it. 'You're nothing but a bunch of scoundrels and cowards. You should be preparing the details of the insurrection. I'll make sure you're all punished', et cetera.

INESSA

He's in one of his rages. I can see why . . . I think he should return soon. Without him . . .

NADYA

He will, he will. Don't worry . . .

(Inessa blushes)

INESSA

It's not what I meant.

NADYA

I know. Have you heard about KOLLONTAI?

INESSA

Yes. The first woman member of the Central Committee.
Miracles will never cease.

NADYA

Your name was mentioned too, as was mine, but
Volodya was not in favour. We pay a price, my dear
comrade.

INT/EXT. VILLAGE. FINLAND – EVENING

*Lenin in a hut. A young Bolshevik messenger is waiting. He
has just finished a letter.*

LENIN
(writing and reading)
'Comrades, I'm very touched by your solicitude, but I'm
on my way back. Our trusted friend who brought me
here will bring me back. Lenin'
    Hand this to Comrade SVERDLOV. And be careful. If
you feel you're being followed, destroy the letter but
memorise it. Simple enough.

*Lenin is changing into his disguise when engine driver
arrives and watches approvingly.*

ENGINE-DRIVER

Pity you lost your hair, Vladimir Ilyich. Make you look
so much younger.

They leave the hut. Lenin is wearing railway worker outfit.

LENIN
Better I lost it my friend. Otherwise, they wouldn't be able to call me Starich.

INT. PRISON. ST PETERSBURG – DAY

Kresty prison. Trotsky, Kamenev, Kronstadt sailors and several others mull their fate.

TROTSKY
General Kornilov is marching on Petersburg. Kerensky is now appealing to us to support him.

SAILOR
Let Kornilov hang the bastard.

KAMENEV
Better the other way round. But if we have to, we must defend the Soviet against the general.

TROTSKY
When a counterrevolutionary general is throwing a noose round the neck of the Soviet, the sailors of Kronstadt must defend the Soviet. Let's defeat Kornilov first, then we'll deal with Kerensky.

SAILOR
You know what my mates think of both these fucking K's, but I'll tell them what you said, Comrade Trotsky.

Lawyer enters with police. They have all been granted bail. They embrace.

TROTSKY
(to Kamenev)
Our agitators in the Army will defeat Kornilov. His soldiers
will desert him. I'm sure of this. We won't need to fire a shot.

EXT. TINY RAILWAY STATION – DAY

*Engine-Driver gets into his cabin and pulls Lenin up behind
him. Steam envelops the platform as train pulls out.*

LENIN
I hope this will be the last time.

(as the train gathers speed)

ENGINE-DRIVER
You're sure it's safe?

LENIN
For me? Yes. For the capitalists? No.

ENGINE-DRIVER
You sure, comrade?

LENIN
The tide has turned. Kerensky, on his knees in front of
the capitalists, and the generals are now appealing to us
for help.

ENGINE-DRIVER
He needs a kicking up his arse, comrade, if you'll forgive
the expression. That's the help we should give him.

(Lenin smiles)

EXT/INT. MILITARY GHQ. ST PETERSBURG – DAY

Car driving Guchkov and Miliukov stops outside. The two men in coattails and hats walk through the parade ground where soldiers are lounging, smoking, chatting.

An Agitator is recounting the bean story and illustrating it. There is a pyramid of beans with Tsar on the top. Just another bean. The agitator slaps the pyramid lightly and the structure collapses.

AGITATOR

Now can anyone find the Tsar?

> (laughter and cheers. Then he recognises the two men, whispers, and they are surrounded)

What can we do for a pair of such fine ladies? So well dressed. Look at their silk hats. Where do you get the money from? Come to see the general? He's there, waiting for you.

> (waves to the window)

General, your friends are here.

SOLDIER I

It's no use, gentlemen. We'll never fight against our own. Just like you.

AGITATOR

The Black Hundreds won't be enough. Nor will the monks. You'll have to hire mercenaries from abroad to kill Russian workers and soldiers.

SOLDIER 2

Now, killing them will be a pleasure.

(laughter)

General KORNILOV, *seeing all this from a window, comes down with an aide.*

Soldiers with sullen expressions ignore him. Those standing sit down again and start playing cards.

Kornilov is livid. But takes his two guests upstairs to his office. Two officers click their heels, salute the party, and open the door.

GUCHKOV

God in heaven. I had no idea things were so bad.

MILIUKOV

Kerensky promised but couldn't deliver. But nor could you, General.

KORNILOV

Had I attempted to do so, we would all have been wiped out. We tried in July. We failed.

MILIUKOV

Are we going to wait till we're blotted out? They tell me Lenin's on the way back.

KORNILOV

We should have hanged all the scoundrels we put in prison. All those bloody Jews.

MILIUKOV

The time has gone, but after the entente with the Americans has defeated Germany . . .

KORNILOV

You'll ask them to come here and get rid of the yids?

GUCHKOV

Of the Bolsheviks, General. I am in regular contact with the British Ambassador. There is hope yet . . .

KORNILOV

Our people will not like foreign armies on our soil. They never do.

MILIUKOV

They will if the Tsar and the Church tell them it's necessary.

KORNILOV

I'm not sure. We will have to create a new army with the Tsar at its head. Russians to win back Holy Russia. The foreigners can fight separately or at least be seen to do so.

GUCHKOV

The British have refused to send a ship to take the Tsar and his family to safety in England. King George was sympathetic but his ministers said a very loud no.

MILIUKOV

Britain, too, is divided. The Revolution has many supporters there and the Labour Party is keen to send a delegation to the Soviet. The rest of Europe won't be different. Our situation is dire, but there have been mutinies in the British, French and German armies, too. On a small scale, I agree. But we face a difficult task.

GUCHKOV

What if the moderate socialists defeat the Bolsheviks?

MILIUKOV

That will not happen. All our agents report a huge shift in the direction of Lenin and Trotsky. And these two have no equivalent in the moderate ranks.

GUCHKOV

Pity you didn't become a moderate socialist.

KORNILOV

There is only one solution. Annihilation. We must prepare. In the forests, in the churches, in the cold, in the dark till the scourge is exterminated and our country cleansed. If we had succeeded in July . . .

MILIUKOV

But you failed.

INT/EXT. BOLSHEVIK HQ – DAY

Lenin and Engine-Driver arrive. Guards fail to recognise them. Lenin lifts the wig. The guards gasp. He hands them the wig, and both men enter the building.

'Comrade Lenin is back' reverberates and the door to the central committee room opens.

Stalin and Kamenev come to greet him. He throws off his coat, and they walk to the room where the Central Committee meeting is waiting. He is greeted warmly by some.

LENIN

I warned you'd be arrested if you stayed.

(laughter)

So where are we? I hope at the final stages of planning to take power? No? You surprise me.

SVERDLOV

Welcome back. Some of us didn't appreciate the abusive letter.

LENIN

Where is it? Was I too intemperate?

KAMENEV

We burnt it. Had we been raided that letter would have been headline news: LENIN DECLARES ALL HIS CENTRAL COMMITTEE CONSISTS OF SCOUNDRELS AND COWARDS.

(laughter)

LENIN

I didn't mean all of you.

KAMENEV

We know who you meant. Some of us don't agree with you. We feel at the present time we have to unite with the moderates and present a united block against Kornilov.

LENIN

Your tactics were correct for July. Disastrous for October.

SVERDLOV

The attempted counterrevolution shook the Mensheviks and the others. They still don't know what is to be done, but they agreed to setting up a Military Revolutionary

Committee. Comrade Trotsky as Chairman of the Soviet is also Chairman of the Committee.

TROTSKY

The proposal came from an eighteen-year-old kid. A Left SR. We accepted. And after a debate the Soviet agreed. It could be a useful instrument. Perhaps even a decisive one.

SVERDLOV

Good. Comrade Lenin will report on the political and military situation.

LENIN

We have reached the most critical moment of the revolution. Its future depends on us. We can no longer blame the moderates for dragging their feet.

The changed mood is reflected in the fact we have won majorities in the Petrograd and Moscow Soviets and in several other cities.

The chart is pinned on the wall outside. That is why Comrade Trotsky is the Chairman of the Soviet here. There are at least three Bolshevik regiments in this city. Why are they voting for us? What are we going to do with these majorities? Are we going to dissipate this support?

Peasant uprisings have been reported in several areas. Even the bourgeoisie recognise that, as far as we are concerned, the war is lost. Guchkov spends most of his time in the British Embassy.

History never offers the oppressed too many chances. If we turn our backs on this one, generations of revolutionaries will curse us in times to come. What I am proposing will not surprise any of you, I hope. We have no option but to prepare to take power. No time for niceties.

I'm not saying we start here. The armed insurrection could be launched in Moscow or even Finland and converge on Petrograd. If we delay, the enemy will launch another assault. We must pre-empt their offensive by launching our own, in our name and taking full responsibility for our actions. I suggest that we set a date for the insurrection. I'm sure the majority of the country is waiting for us to take decisive action.

There are gasps of surprise. Zinoviev is livid. Kamenev is trembling. Others nervous. Trotsky deep in thought.

SVERDLOV

Kamenev has the floor.

KAMENEV

I am totally opposed to this adventurism. It will be a bloody debacle. Conditions are not yet ripe. We will be isolated and destroyed and future generations will curse us for acting out of turn. The majority of the country is not with us as yet. I ask this Committee to warn all party organisations against insurrectionism. Lenin is playing with fire.

LENIN

And you Kamenev are a Skoptsy not a Bolshevik!

(some laugh, others are shocked. Trotsky impassive)

SVERDLOV

Order. I recognise Comrade Trotsky.

TROTSKY

I agree with Comrade Lenin. We have to set a date. We have to organise an armed insurrection. We have to take power. A dual power cannot exist in a country for ever. The enemy knows that full well. Sooner or later a choice has to be made.

My difference with Lenin is purely tactical. I think the insurrection should be in the name of the Congress of Soviets, *not* the party. Everything else stands as argued by Lenin. Simply that the Soviet carries it out. This should take care of Kamenev's fear of isolation.

We will organise the insurrection, take power and hand it to the Congress of Soviets. That is *our* parliament.

(many are nodding)

LENIN

What if the Mensheviks refused to convene the congress?

TROTSKY

We will do so ourselves. Most of us are agreed on the ends. The means are not unimportant. We must take as many with us as we can.

SVERDLOV

I am about to adjourn the Central Committee.

KAMENEV

I insist my motion is put to the vote. 'We warn all party organisations against insurrectionism.'

SVERDLOV

No more speeches. All in favour of this motion?

Zinoviev and Kamenev raise their hands.

Against?

A majority including Lenin and Trotsky.

We will reconvene tomorrow.

INT. INESSA'S APARTMENT. KITCHEN – NIGHT

Lenin is drinking tea. Inessa is massaging his shoulders.

INESSA

Kollontai told me what you said.

LENIN

What did I say?

INESSA

Don't play the innocent with me. You called Kamenev a
Skoptsy.

LENIN
(smiling, turns round and hugs her)
He is a political Skoptsy.

INESA

Volchik! Did the committee men even know what you
were talking about?

LENIN

Stalin will explain it to them. He was a seminary
student.

INESSA

First, unlike Zinoviev and Kamenev, the Skoptsy were fanatics. They castrated themselves so they could live saintly lives in religious communes.

LENIN

Enough. Agreed that Zinoviev and Kamenev are not fanatics. But confronted with a weak bourgeoisie they want to castrate themselves.

INESSA

You're the fanatic. Perhaps I should castrate you.

LENIN

You tried and failed.

INESSA
(kisses his cheeks)
Are you sure this is the time to strike.

LENIN
(eyes cold and distant)
Never been so sure of anything in my life.

INT. THE WINTER PALACE – DAY

Premier Kerensky and Miliukov.

MILIUKOV

Unless you do something now, we're lost.

KERENSKY

What do you suggest?

MILIUKOV

Dissolve the Soviet by force of arms.

KERENSKY

And create a military dictatorship.

MILIUKOV

No. Temporary military rule while we organise elections to the Duma.

KERENSKY

And return to the days of Stolypin and Rasputin. Impossible. How out of touch you've become. Leave it to me. Your plutocrats have failed. I will outmanoeuvre the Soviet but in my own way.

MILIUKOV
(white with anger)

You're a joke. That's what you are. A braggart without brains.

(Walks out)

EXT. ODESSA. MOLDOVANKA, THE
JEWISH QUARTER – EVENING.

A pogrom in progress.

INT/EXT. THE SOVIET IN SESSION.
25 SEPTEMBER 1917 – DAY.

Packed, tense chamber.

Comrades, as we gather the country is in turmoil. There have been hunger riots in Zhitomir, Kharkov, Tambov, Orel and Odessa. Yes, Odessa. The military has responded with repression. Shootings, killing and savage pogroms. In the face of all this, Kerensky has set up a new Provisional Government . . .

(cries of 'imbecile', 'braggart')

. . . that consists of people who support these crimes. This is the government of civil war. A dictatorship of the bourgeoisie that even the most intelligent bourgeois holds in contempt. He would prefer a straightforward military dictatorship to turn their guns on our people.

I have a simple resolution: 'We, the workers and garrison of Petersburg, refuse to support the government of bourgeois autocracy and counterrevolutionary violence. We express the unshakable conviction that the new government will meet with a single response from the entire revolutionary democracy: *resign.*'

(applause, shouts of *Yes, resign. Resign*)

I put the motion to the vote.
    For.

(an overwhelming majority raise their hands)

The vote is clear. We shall now organise and see how best to overthrow this filthy government.

(applause)

As Trotksy leaves many come forward to slap him on the back. He suddenly sees Martov observing him with a sardonic smile. They shake hands, and Trotsky pulls him up and drags him out.

Both of them laugh silently and walk out to a café. Many greet them as they walk. The cafés are packed, so the two men find an empty bench and occupy it.

MARTOV

I know what's going on. Lenin and you are preparing an armed insurrection. Zinoviev and Kamenev are opposed, and the leadership of this great party is nervous. Some say, 'Lenin's gone mad.' It's not true. But he's in one of his rages, this time against our common enemy. I mean the bourgeoisie, not poor old Kamenev.

TROTSKY

So, the rumour factories are working overtime. Let me tell you that the Soviet and its Military Revolutionary Committee will decide when and what.

MARTOV

Bwisyt. Bobe-Mayse as my father used to say. Bullshit. You control the Soviet. Without the Bolsheviks the Military Revolutionary Committee would be nothing. So you will decide and the Soviet will stamp its approval.

TROTSKY

So cynical!

MARTOV

Such a good Bolshevik boy. Who would have guessed. Certainly not Lenin. Oh. A hit, a hit. That annoyed you.

TROTSKY

You've lost your own party. The Elders—

MARTOV

The shysters.

TROTSKY

So why not join us and isolate the shysters. But no. It hurts your pride. Yes, I was the same as you. I know. And I was wrong. Wasted a lot of time. You have to admit Lenin was right on the party and on the revolution.

MARTOV

During the old *Iskra* days, I was closer to him than anyone else. I still feel close, but I don't trust him.

TROTSKY

Is that why you didn't come back on the train, but waited till the shysters gave you permission and then the Germans gave you a train? Anyway, the point is this – that this is not the time to reduce the rise of new social forces on a historical scale to individual relationships.

MARTOV

It's not the revolution I fear, but the aftermath. What are the guarantees that —

TROTSKY

You're like a bride-to-be who, even before the marriage, is obsessed by the divorce.

She knows the marriage is forced. Even if she survives the first few months, she'll be raped for the rest of her life.

Unbeknown to them, Kollontai has crept close and eavesdropped

KOLLONTAI

Marriage, divorce, rape. What are you two talking about?

TROTSKY

You take over. Convince him to join our ranks.

(to Martov) We will resume the conversation.

MARTOV

In better circumstances or worse?

Trotsky walks away deep in thought. As he is walking, he's approached by a group of sailors. An animated conversation.

EXT./INT – DAY.

A montage to illustrate Inessa's VO

INESSA (VO)

All the debates within the Central Committee would have been of no avail without the members of the party. Its agitators in the army and navy. Its leaders in the factories. In every form of mass activity, they were there every day working stubbornly and without a pause.

This no party Left or Right could imitate, for in the months between late July and October the Bolsheviks had been assimilated by the masses as their own people. Their only hope. Without this there could not have been a Bolshevik majority in the main Soviets and no revolution.

Lenin understood better than all the others that the masses would follow the Bolsheviks with or without anyone else in tow. It was for this reason that he asked for a secret meeting with Trotsky. The government still refused to withdraw the arrest orders for Lenin. Officially he was still underground but came out of hiding for important meetings.

INT. INESSA'S KITCHEN – DAY

Lenin and Trotsky alone across the table. Lenin stands up and paces up and down.

LENIN

Of course I understand what you're doing. Soviet legality and Soviet constitutionalism is dear to me as well, but not if it becomes a fetish and we fail to seize the time. Timing in politics is crucial. Much more for us than the bourgeoisie. They have a world already and they will appeal to it for help. That is my only worry Lev Davidovich.

TROTSKY

Nothing divides us. Nothing. I hope you appreciate this fact. If the Mensheviks try to delay, we will vote our own resolution through. Your analysis is totally correct. Two days ago, a few sailors from Kronstadt approached me. They are ready. Give the word, they said, and we will take over the fortress and give the signal for the

Sailors Soviet to take the navy. So let us set the date at the next Central Committee.

LENIN

Kollontai tells me you were trying to win over Martov. Any luck?

TROTSKY

He's the Hamlet of socialism. Can never make up his mind. On a personal level too.

LENIN

Hamlet, yes. Zinoviev and Kamenev are Rosencrantz and Guildenstern, or is it the other way round?

(both men smile)

TROTSKY

I told Martov how much I regretted having wasted so much time outside the party. And why one mustn't let pride stand in the way.

LENIN

On this too we are in agreement. Did he reply?

TROTSKY

He said that both of you were very close during the *Iskra* days. That he still feels very close to you but doesn't trust you.

LENIN
(shouts)

He doesn't trust *me!* Outrageous. The question is does he still feel close to the revolution? Why can't he break with this bunch of murderous intriguers? Why does he . . .? It doesn't matter . . .

Hmm. Hamlet, Rosencrantz, and Guildenstern on the same Central Committee might be trouble.

(Trotsky smiles)

There are three other matters we need to discuss before the Central Committee reconvenes . . .

INT. THE SOVIET IN SESSION.
10 OCTOBER 1917 – DAY

Trotsky presiding. He recognises a SOLDIER *delegate.*

SOLDIER
Comrades, I was informed last night that the officers are preparing to move our regiments out of the city. They say the German army is poised to seize our capital and rather than organise its defence, they want to shift to Moscow.

(pandemonium in hall)

TROTSKY
Order. Comrades, I propose we adjourn this session, so we can have an emergency meeting of the Military Revolutionary Committee that you have set up to combat the counterrevolution.

As delegates pour out, Stalin rushes towards Trotsky.

STALIN
Vladimir Ilyich has asked the Central Committee to reconvene tonight.

(hands Trotsky a piece of paper)

This is the address.

                    TROTSKY
                    (laughs)
But this is Sukhanov's house. Does he know? Or has he
come over?

                    STALIN
                    (whisper)
No. His wife's a Bolshevik. She'll keep him out tonight.

EXT. RIVER BANK. ST PETERSBURG – AFTERNOON

Inessa, Nadya and Kollontai are walking. Boats on the river.

                    KOLLONTAI
As you know, the boats are going to be burnt tonight.
Have you seen him?

(Inessa shakes her head. Kollontai gives her as sly smile]

                    NADYA
I saw him a few hours ago.

                    KOLLONTAI
And?

                    (Nadya smiles but says nothing]

                    INESSA
The Moscow party is sending angry messages demanding action. It seems they're prepared.

Everyone is prepared except two of our generals. They tried to canvas me to vote against.

INESSA

Kamenev is Trotsky's brother-in-law. Can't our great orator convince him?

NADYA

Not as easy as you think. If Ilyich can't convince them, nobody will.

EXT./INT. PRIVATE HOUSE. KARPOVKA. CENTRAL COMMITTEE IN SESSION – NIGHT.

The mood is tense. Each arrives separately and enters the house. Ten present. Lenin arrives with wig but no beard. Zinoviev with beard but shaved head. On the face of it they appear calm. Trotsky enters the room and takes an empty place.
  Sverdlov calls the meeting to order.

TROTSKY

Comrades, the Military Revolutionary Committee decided that any attempt to transfer three regiments, the ones that we control, out of the city will be resisted. There is no doubt Kornilov and his fellow Generals are preparing another assault. They, too, have realized that Kerensky is utterly useless. I think we have no option but to set the date for the insurrection.

Pin-drop silence. Zinoviev and Kamenev become agitated. Lenin raises his hand and is recognised.

We are ready to defend our revolution against the Germans or the Entente. We are not prepared to put our soldiers and sailors in the hands of Kerensky or Kornilov, whose only aim now is to destroy the revolution.

You have in front of you the resolution passed by the Second Congress of the sailors of the Baltic Fleet. The words are harsh, the sentiments are clear. They want the end of this government.

We have had many differences on this question, but I would advise comrades to accept that there is now no other choice. If we delay further, we become part of the problem. The relationship of forces is now in our favour.

I understand fully the arguments against, but what should not be underestimated is that if we triumph, Europe will follow. Without a revolution in Germany, we might not be able to last too long, but the sailors mutiny in Kiel, the unrest in Berlin indicates a pre-revolutionary crisis.

Our revolution is only the beginning of a process.

ZINOVIEV

Before history, before the international proletariat, before the Russian revolution and our working class, we have no right to stake the entire future on a single card: an armed uprising. The dangers are too great. It will end in a debacle that will spill far more blood than the Paris Commune.

There are historical situations when an oppressed class recognises that is better to be defeated than not to fight.

Do Russian workers confront such a situation? No! A thousand times no.

Lenin says we can never be sure. First engage, he says, then we'll see. He quotes Napoleon whose own career—

TROTSKY

You overestimate the strength of our enemies at home and underestimate the strength of the European prole-tariat. Our revolution will be the prelude to the German revolution. Lenin's resolution makes this very clear. The motive for an armed insurrection is the 'international situation of the Russian Revolution, the revolt in the German navy is an extreme manifestation of the growth throughout Europe of the world socialist revolution.'

KAMENEV

And what if the German workers movement doesn't oblige us? Then what will happen?

LENIN

Let's hope Luxemburg and Liebknecht turn out to be better than you and Zinoviev.

Silent montage of hands raised, angry gestures, different speakers.

SVERDLOV

We move to the vote. For Lenin's motion that sets the date as October 20th. For?

Eight hands rise.

Against?

Zinoviev and Kamenev.

Two.
 Comrade Lenin's resolution is carried.

The meeting disperses. Lenin and Trotsky leave. Others fall
to the floor and put the lights out.
Outside Lenin and Trotsky breathe the air.

LENIN

You are sure?

TROTSKY

Why do you doubt? Everything is ready. I'm convinced
we will take Petersburg and Moscow without too many
problems.

LENIN

They will not fight.

TROTSKY

Not here. Perhaps a token struggle in Moscow.

LENIN

I hope you're right.

The two men shake hands and part.

INT./EXT. A MONTAGE. FACTORY. GARRISON. CROWD

Kollontai, Trotsky others, speaking to crowds.
Lenin writing.
Stalin producing the newspaper.

INESSA (VO)

The last ten days before the revolution, none of us had
time to speak to each other. Rosencrantz and
Guildenstern had gone public and published the Central
Committee plans and their opposition in Gorky's

newspaper. Volchik was in one his rages, demanding they be expelled from the Committee. But he could not win a majority and got angry with Trotsky.

INT. INESSA'S KITCHEN – DAY

LENIN

Why did you vote against Zinoviev and Kamenev's expulsion from the Committee?

TROTSKY

I think it's wrong on principle but more important than that is the timing. They are seen as your closest comrades and veterans of the party. It would create confusion in the ranks if we weren't united on the eve of insurrection. The base of the party is still confused.

LENIN

A ruse de guerre?

TROTSKY

One of many.

INT. THE SOVIET. 21 OCTOBER – DAY

A young Bolshevik enters the hall, rushes straight to the platform and whispers in Trotsky's ear.

TROTSKY

I have just received some grave news. The Government has ordered that the Bolshevik Party's newspaper offices be closed till further notice.

Uproar.

Comrades. With your permission I will request the Military Revolutionary Committee dispatch a contingent of armed Red Guards to make sure the offices remain open.

Applause. Trotsky instructs aides.

Comrades, yesterday the MRC sent an instruction to all the regiments. Unless an order is countersigned by us, it should not be obeyed.

Gasps in the Soviet, followed by loud applause.
Martov and colleagues express their anger.

MARTOV
(whispers to colleague)
You can see what they're up to.

COLLEAGUE I
Yes, I can, but so can the government. Which side will you be on?

INT./EXT. WINTER PALACE.
KERENSKY'S OFFICE – DAY

Kerensky and ministers in session. COSSACK COMMANDER *of the Garrison is heading for the palace in command car. He gets out and walks to the meeting room.*

KERENSKY
We have been waiting.

COSSACK COMMANDER
Nothing important to report.

KERENSKY

I told you. The situation is under control.

COSSACK COMMANDER

The Bolsheviks are preparing a demonstration of protest against the government. I asked Trotsky, 'Will your workers be armed?' He said, 'Yes.'

KERENSKY

Ever since their own leaders published the date of their so-called insurrection, there has been nothing to fear. Trotsky cannot be trusted, but he's not a fool. But in case this demonstration gets out of hand, can you, er . . .

COSSACK COMMANDER

We have everything under control.

He salutes. They smile to reassure each other. Cossack Commander leaves the room.

INT. ROOM – DAY

Lenin writing as Stalin waits.

LENIN

Rejection of the insurrection is little more than placing one's confidence in the bourgeoisie and the vacillators to deliver something. There is no middle way. Either 'All power to the Soviets' or loyalty to the Constituent assembly, to Rodzianko, to Kerensky and watch as they surrender Petersburg and smother the revolution.

The only path left to us is insurrection. We must now agitate for it in public. Martov and his cronies accuse us of a coup d'état, but we are not conspiring in secret. We

74

are saying openly and publicly to the workers and soldiers of Russia: it is time to take power.

Here you are. Tomorrow's edition.

Hands it to Stalin, who takes it and leaves.

EXT – LATE AFTERNOON.

Kollontai and Inessa

KOLLONTAI

The news is good. Everywhere in the provinces, in the Soviets, we are dominant. On this there are no disputes. When we strike there will be support all over the country.

INESSA

What if they strike first? They haven't disappeared you know. They will fight.

KOLLONTAI

They are hampered by the war. The most reactionary regiments under their command are on the front. They have no time to divert them now. Too late. Too late. And, and even from the front, from units big and small, Bolshevik resolutions are being passed and sent to the Soviet.

INESSA

I heard you say that the other day at the Cirque. It was an excellent speech.

KOLLONTAI

Never easy speaking after Trotsky. He's a magician. I have to go.

They embrace and Kollontai runs away.

And the letters I'm getting from Moscow are amazing.
Volchik always used to say, even years ago, that mass
consciousness is never linear. It can go up very fast and
then, if nothing happens, it can come down even more
rapidly. But something is going to happen.

EXT. MOSCOW. HUGE DEMONSTRATION. 18 OCTOBER 1917

*Several thousand on the streets, with uniformed soldiers the
most dominant element. Kremlin in background. Agitators
carrying little stools are accompanying the march. The mood
is angry and impatient.*

*The banner leading the demonstration, carried by soldiers
reads: 'WE WOULD RATHER DIE IN MOSCOW ON
THE BARRICADES THAN GO TO THE FRONT!'*

*'The Marseillaise' is sung, but a group of marchers drown
it out with a newer song, 'The Internationale'. The words
are passed around.*

AGITATOR

And, comrades, let us send a loud message to comrades
Lenin and Trotsky in Petersburg. What are you waiting
for? We are ready. Give the command and we will take
Moscow.

(loud applause)
(chants: *Insurrection, Insurrection, Revolution*)
(all sing 'The Internationale')

INT. THE SOVIET, SMOLNY.
21 OCTOBER 1917 – DAY

Regimental and company committees from all the Petersburg military units are assembled.

TROTSKY
Comrades, we invited you so we could hear your views on the situation inside the garrison.

SOLDIER
I am from the Pavlovsky. Other delegates have come from the Ismailovsky, Chasseurs, Volhynians,

(as he names them the delegates acknowledge their presence]

Grenadiers, Cuxholms, Semyonovskys, Rifles, the Electro-Technical Battalion, the Moscow Regiment, the 89th.
I'm getting tired. In other words, we are all here. Others will speak for themselves. The Pavlovskys have decided. We obey the Soviet. When you give the call to get rid of this government we will come out.

Applause. Others repeat what he said and the applause grows.

CAVALRY DELEGATE
Citizens, I am from the Cavalry Regiment. We remain neutral so far.

(understanding nods from others)

Thank you, comrade delegates. We expected nothing else from you. There are three resolutions before us. The Congress of Soviets is about to take power in order to secure Peace, Bread and Land for all our people.

Do you pledge to place all your forces at the disposal of the Soviets?

Can we vote?

The vote is overwhelming. Nem. con.

The only authority whose orders should be followed is the Military Revolutionary Committee of the Soviet.

The vote is unchanged.

Tomorrow we are planning a huge demonstration. A peaceful show of strength. Will you watch over us and ensure that any provocation by the bourgeoisie will be resisted?

Same vote. Session ends.
Sailors rush over to Trotsky.

KRONSTADT SAILOR

Comrade Trotsky, we are planning to take over the base tonight and remove our commanders. Do we have your permission?

TROTSKY

Yes, lock them up, but no violence.

KRONSTADT SAILOR

Don't know what the word means, comrade.

INT. WINTER PALACE

Kerensky and Cossack Commander.

> KERENSKY
>
> Two days ago, you told me . . . do you remember what you told me? Do you mind repeating it to the Prime Minister of your government.

> COSSACK COMMANDER
>
> There is no reason to think that the garrison will refuse to obey the orders of the military authorities.

> KERENSKY
> (angry)
>
> Is that still your view?

> COSSACK COMMANDER
>
> It is, Prime Minister.

> KERENSKY
>
> You may go.

Cossack Commander salutes and leaves.

INT. THE SOVIET. SMOLNY – DAY

In session. Messengers coming in and out. Orders being signed. Trotsky listening intently and anxiously to a Commissar.

> TROTSKY
>
> This comrade has arrived from Peter and Paul. The Commandant refused to accept our authority.

ANTONOV

Send in the Pavlovskys to disarm the garrison.

TROTSKY

If we do that, we'll have to take the Winter Palace as
well. We need more time. Why don't I go to Peter and
Paul and address the garrison. It will be seen as a
disarming gesture.

We are not about to harm their bodies, just to raise
and win their spirit.

They agree. Trotsky, the Commissar and two others exit.

ANTONOV

Send a few Red Guards with him, just in case.

INT./EXT. THE WINTER PALACE – NIGHT

*Cabinet meeting. Ministers are shaken, on the edge of
collapse. Kerensky in denial.*

MINISTER

If the Bolsheviks have taken Peter and Paul without a
shot being fired, we're finished. A hundred thousand
more rifles are in the hands of these swine.

KERENSKY

Stay calm, Chernov. I am about to go and speak to the
General Staff. Enough's enough. We will decapitate the
serpent tomorrow. Take him unawares.

*They look at each other in despair as Kerensky leaves the
room.*

*Kerensky rushes through the palace, jumps into the wait-
ing car and is driven through empty streets to the military*

HQ. *As car enters, the driver switches off the headlights.*
The car glides to a halt.

INT. MILITARY GHQ – NIGHT

Several uniformed generals and their aides rise and stand to
attention as Kerensky enters. Map of St Petersburg on the
wall with red flags planted on key installations and areas
under Soviet authority.

KERENSKY

We strike tomorrow. We still have ordinary people on
our side. Give the call for volunteers, for a popular
detachment to fight the Soviet. The moderate, middle
classes will rally to us. Here is the necessary government
order.

COSSACK COMMANDER
(reading in disbelief)

'In view of their illegal activities, all Commissars of the
Petersburg Soviet to be removed. All illegal activities by
soldiers and sailors to be investigated by a court
martial . . .'

Prime Minister, take a look at the map. Who is going
to implement this order? It's too late now and too early
for a civil war. All we request is to ask your friends
among the people to allow us to requisition their cars
for military purposes. Of course, we will attempt to
carry out your orders.

They salute him. Kerensky leaves. They burst out
laughing.

COSSACK COMMANDER

Send a message to General Kornilov. Petersburg is about to fall to the Bolsheviks. We await further orders.

EXT. OUTSIDE SMOLNY. 24 OCTOBER – DAY

Trotsky and Antonov are on their way to the MRC.

TROTSKY

Cars still on the roads. It appears Kerensky's appeal doesn't impress his friends.

ANTONOV

There's only one reason the Generals want the cars.

TROTSKY/ANTONOV

To make a quick getaway.

(they laugh)

INT./EXT. SMOLNY. 24 OCTOBER – DAY

MRC in action. Messenger rushes in. Whispers to Antonov, who interrupts Trotsky.

TROTSKY

The Cadets have sealed off two Bolshevik papers. Is this a joke? Yes, it is a joke, but it will prove to be an expensive one for the comedian.

Antonov, take a contingent of Red Guards to reopen the offices. If the Cadets open fire, you have the authority to shoot back in return. Where are the men from the Baltic fleet?

Two sailors are brought to him. They shift to a smaller room.

We have two torpedo boats in the harbour. The entire
Fleet supports the insurrection. Our officers are disarmed
and don't look too unhappy. Your orders for tomorrow
morning are clear. The *Aurora* will fire the cannon.
Comrade, will we see Comrade Lenin tomorrow?

TROTSKY

You will my friend. You will.

*Trotsky embraces each of the sailors in turn. They leave.
Trotsky walks out of the building, taking Antonov with
him. It's chilly. Both men shiver.*

TROTSKY

Go to Lenin. Tell him he we have decided. Tomorrow.
When he hears the cannon fire, we will already be in
command. Tell him the soldiers and sailors want to see
him as the Congress of Soviets assembles. Tell him, we
have won. He was right.

*As Trotsky lights a cigarette, he sees Martov coming in his
direction and frowns.*

MARTOV

When is the holy date? Or has the Lord of the Hosts not
yet decided? When is Jupiter going to descend. Lev
Davidovich, it is still not too late.

TROTSKY
(livid)

For what? Compromise with whom? Can't you see there
is no third way? It's either them or us, with a few old
women like yourself standing and watching.

You've become utterly pathetic. A parody of Hamlet.

83

We're already in the middle of an insurrection, man.
Can't you even see that . . . wake up, Martov. Wake up.

He walks away in anger.

INT. LENIN'S HIDING PLACE. 24 OCTOBER

Lenin is alone. Pacing up and down. Talking to himself.

LENIN

What if the Germans don't follow us? They will. They
will. The sailors mutiny cracked their state apparatus.
We need two uprisings. Berlin. Munich. The rest of the
country will follow.

Must write the first decrees of Soviet power. The Peace
Decree. The Land Decree. Yes. Should do it now so they
can be published the day after tomorrow.

The first hundred days are crucial. We will be judged
by what we do, not what we say.

What if there's no uprising in Germany? Impossible.
There will be. There must be. There has to be.

*He sits down. He stands up. Paces again. Sits down again
and starts writing the decree on Peace. He writes.*

The new Russian government has with immediate effect
withdrawn from the war. This carnage that has gone
on . . .

A messenger arrives. Hands Lenin a note.

LENIN

It's too quiet today. What's going on out there? Take me
to Smolny. Now!

EXT. THE NEVA. 25 OCTOBER 1917

Sailors on the Aurora *rushing to and fro. Cannons are ready.*

Commissar orders 'Fire'.

Soldiers and sailors in all the installations raise the red flag and march out triumphantly. Antonov leads regiments to take the major districts, including the Finland Station. There is no resistance.

A crowd is assembling and chanting, 'To the Winter Palace'.

INT. SMOLNY. THE SOVIET IN SESSION

Trotsky is about to declare the session open. Hubbub. Excitement.

TROTSKY

In the name of the Military Revolutionary Committee of the Petersburg Soviet, I have to inform you that the Provisional Government no longer exists.

Applause. Delegates are singing 'The Internationale'. Trotsky calls them to order.

TROTSKY

No blood has been spilt today. We have not yet taken the Winter Palace but that will happen very soon.

Comrades, we are about to build a new State that will be an instrument of the people and will liberate them from all forms of bondage. We have a comrade waiting to address you, the man most responsible for creating the political force so necessary in preparing the way for this glorious day. He came last night to Smolny to make

sure there was no last-minute compromise. I give you
Comrade Lenin.

*Huge applause as Lenin makes his way to the podium. Then
pin-drop silence as he begins to speak.*

LENIN
We shall now proceed to construct the socialist order.

(applause that he acknowledges and then stops)

The oppressed masses must create their own
Government, their own state. The old state must be
destroyed root and branch and a Soviet form of organisation created to replace the old administrative
apparatus.
    But first things first. We must end the war at once. No
delays. We must annihilate landed property. The workers
must control the industries in which they work. They
know how to run them better than the frauds and
bloodsuckers who own them . . .

(sustained applause)

EXT./INT. THE SAME DAY. WINTER PALACE.

The Aurora *is firing blanks at the palace. Outside a proletarian crowd is getting larger.*
    *Inside the ministers are in a state of nervous collapse.
Kerensky disappears and re-emerges dressed as a cleaning
woman. They look at him in horror. He gives them a pathetic
wave and disappears.*
    *The cadets defending the Winter Palace fire a few shots
out of nervousness. It's the signal for the offensive.*
    Armed Red Guards enter the palace and fire at the cadets,

who run or surrender. The masses enter the palace and occupy it.

Outside a Red Flag flies. Petersburg has fallen to the revolution.

INT. THE SOVIET. SMOLNY – EVENING

A messenger rushes in. Trotsky reads the note handed to him.

TROTSKY

Comrades, the Winter Palace has fallen. Kerensky has fled. The city belongs to the Soviet.

MARTOV

We demand, we demand a government in which the Mensheviks are represented.

TROTSKY

Most of your party has gone over to the other side. You stand here and whine. We reply *no*. You accused us of fomenting bloodshed. Where is it? The masses took the city and the Palace.

MARTOV

It was a conspiracy. You tricked the masses. You've usurped the power of the Soviet.

TROTSKY

The uprising has been successful. It was an insurrection, not a conspiracy. One day you will learn the difference.

You tell us, 'Renounce your victory, yield, compromise.' With whom? Miserable little groups who represent nothing anymore. You are politically bankrupt.

Your role is played out. Go where you belong, into the dustbin of history.

Martov looks shattered as he and his followers leave the hall.
   Lenin, his eyes angry, nods vigorously at Trotsky.
   In the gallery, Inessa looks at him and smiles, desperate for him to see her, but he is otherwise engaged, scribbling decrees on notepaper.

TROTSKY

Comrades, I declare this session closed. We will reassemble tomorrow to ask your approval for a new Soviet government.
   Comrades, the insurrection has been successful. Long live the World Revolution!

The Congress rises and sings 'The Internationale'.

INT. MONTAGE. EMBASSIES SENDING DESPATCHES

Diplomatic cables being sent to Chanceries.

BOLSHEVIKS TAKE OVER GOVERNMENT.

RUSSIA WITHDRAWS FROM THE WAR.

Archive Newsreel.

INT. THE WHITE HOUSE, WASHINGTON, DC

WOODROW WILSON *and colleagues are looking at the map of Europe.*

The disease must not spread. We will have to send more troops to Europe. How long will these guys last?

SECRETARY OF STATE

Difficult to say, Mr President. A few years? Depends on whether Germany goes the same way.

WILSON

Let's defeat it first. Then we'll deal with this new menace.

EXT. THE FRONT. RUSSIA

Cheers as news reaches the soldiers.
German soldiers are bewildered as they see the Russians waving and some withdrawing from the front.

INT. THE WINTER PALACE. THE TSAR'S WINE CELLARS.

A bacchanalia in progress. Soldiers from the Preobrazhensky Regiment look at the vintage wines and decide to taste them. As Antonov describes what is happening to the Politburo, we witness it on the screen.

ANTONOV (VO)

The Pavlovsky Regiment, our rampart, succumbed as well. We sent guards from various regiments. They, too, couldn't resist. We sent men of the armoured brigades to end this bacchanal. Soon they, too, were swaying uneasily on their feet.

At dusk the mad bacchanals would spread. 'Let us finish off these Tsarist remnants,' they would shout as more people entered the cellar.

When we appointed a special Commissar, he couldn't resist the wine either. We sent the fire brigades to flood the cellars. They got drunk instead.

It was only when the sailors arrived from the Baltic fleet and stood firm that this alcoholic lunacy was brought to an end.

INT. INESSA'S BEDROOM – NIGHT

Inessa and Lenin.

> INESSA

Please try and get some sleep.
(she strokes his head)

> LENIN

Three days. Three days they carried on drinking.

> INESSA

At the party school in Paris soon after we were together.

> LENIN

What?

> INESSA

I heard you say that revolutions are festivals of the oppressed and exploited.

> LENIN
> (sitting up in bed)

But not this . . .

> INESSA

So now we need rules that forbid the oppressed from celebrating the revolution as they wish . . .

LENIN
I have more important things to think about.

INESSA

So have I.

She switches off the lamp.

EXT. MOSCOW. STREET. MONTAGE. ARCHIVE.

INESSA (VO)

We tried to make peace. The Germans wanted more and
more territory. The party was split. Fearing that
Petrograd was too vulnerable, the government shifted to
Moscow. Trotsky tried to buy time by delaying the
treaty, but the German High Command had its orders.
Lenin insisted that we sign the treaty to get some breath-
ing space for the people.

Within the Bolsheviks there was anger. The Left
Bolsheviks led by BUKHARIN wanted armed resistance. I
agreed with them. At one point we thought Lenin,
isolated by successive votes in the Central Committee
might resign. That sobered everyone for a while. The
crisis was avoided.

But the German surrender in 1918 produced a new
crisis. The Tsarist Generals backed by Britain and
France launched a war to take back the country.
Trotsky, as Commissar of War, was authorised to create
a new model army: the Red Army. It was in this chaos
that the Social Revolutionaries began a campaign of
terror. Two Bolshevik leaders were assassinated by SR
members.

EXT./INT. HAMMER AND SICKLE
FACTORY. MOSCOW – DAY

Lenin arrives outside the factory in his car. Apart from the chauffeur, he is alone. There is no bodyguard nor is there a reception committee.
He gets out of the car and walks into the factory, where he is greeted by the Bolshevik factory committee. The mood is sombre. He stands on a hastily erected platform.

LENIN

Comrades, I felt it my duty to come directly and report to you on the situation in our country. Our troubles are not over yet. As we attempt to retake territory evacuated by the Germans, the Tsarists have formed three armies to try and defeat us.

They are backed by twenty-two countries, big and small. For them it is a Holy War to take back Holy Russia. But the Russia they fight is not the same they left behind. This is your Russia. A workers and peasants republic.

We will need the most politically conscious amongst you to think hard. We need you in the Red Army that is being built even as I speak with you. We need soldiers who know why they are fighting, and we have to defend our state. Who knows how long we live? What we are building is for your children and their children.

(applause)

WORKER

Comrade Lenin, will there be bread in the Red Army?

(laughter)

92

Lenin smiles and walks over to talk with a group of workers. As they come out, workers surround him for a moment, a few paces from his car.

A woman who has been skulking in the background walks up and fires three shots at him. He is seriously wounded in the neck and shoulder.

Lenin is driven back to the Kremlin.

INT. KREMLIN APARTMENT.

Lenin manages to walk upstairs in silence to the second floor and drops to the ground in deep pain. Doctors rush in. He survives.

Nadya enters, her face distraught.

He regains consciousness as she clutches his hand.

NADYA
Volodya, Volodya. Not like this.

LENIN
Charlotte Corday.

He falls asleep, then sits up in bed and tries to get a glass of water. She rushes forward and gets it for him. Holds the glass while he drinks.

LENIN
Nadya, who knows how long I've got. Please, please ask her to come to me. Forgive me, but I need her.

Nadya nods and settles him down. As she walks out of the room she is weeping silently.

INT. MOSCOW. CROWDED BOHEMIAN CAFÉ

MAYAKOVSKY, BABEL, LISSITZKY, MAYERHOLD *and* EISEN-
STEIN *are sitting at a large table, talking, laughing, drinking.
Inessa and three women are sitting at an adjoining table.
Everyone is waiting for Mayakovsky to recite. Lissitzky
shows his first sketch of the* Beat the Whites with the Red
Wedge.

> MEYERHOLD

Excellent. Use it as a basis for the new set design.

> BABEL

Not another Mayakovsky play!

> MEYERHOLD

No. Eisenstein wants to make a film about *Potemkin*
before taking on *Capital*, but I will beat him to it with a
new play on the revolution and every night we will have
a fresh report from the front where Trotsky's Red Wedge
is tearing the White Armies apart. I thought you were on
the train with him, Babel.

> BABEL

No. I'm joining the Red Army. Proletarians to arms!

> EISENSTEIN

Can I film you on horseback?

> BABEL

Why not film the horse from behind. More your style.

Recite something Volodya. These kids are desperate for you.

Mayakovsky rises and goes to the front.

MAYAKOVSKY

This one is called 'Ode to the Revolution'. If you know it, please don't recite it with me. I prefer my own voice.

(laughter)

What was your other name?
How will you turn around again, two-faced?
slender building,
pile of rubble?
to the machinist,
dusted with coal,
to a miner who breaks through the strata of ores,
swear,
swear reverently
praise human labour.
And tomorrow
blissful
cathedral rafters
vainly lifts up, I pray for mercy,
your six-inch blunt-nosed boars
blow up the millennium of the Kremlin.
'Glory.'
Wheezes on a death flight.
The screech of sirens is strangled thin.
You send sailors
on a sinking cruiser
there,
where is the forgotten

the kitten meowed.
And then!
Drunk crowd screaming.
The dashing moustache is twisted in force.
Butts persecuting grey-haired admirals
upside down
from the bridge in Helsingfors.
Yesterday's wounds lick and lick,
and I see open veins again.
You philistine
– oh, damn you thrice! –

While he is reciting, a young woman enters and rushes straight to Inessa. She whispers in her ear. Inessa almost faints. She whispers to one of her friends. Then she rushes out of the café.

Babel has heard the name 'Lenin' mentioned. Mayakovsky stops reciting and comes back to the table.

BABEL
(to neighbouring woman)
What's happened? Why did Inessa rush out?

Woman whispers in his ear. He's stunned. All the women at the next table leave.

There's been an attempt on Lenin's life. He's badly wounded.

MAYAKOVSKY
(screams)
No! No!

He stands up on the table.

The counterrevolutionaries have shot Lenin, but he will live. One way or the other, he will live. That I know. He will live. The revolution will live. Let us sing. Loudly so he might hear us in the Kremlin.

The whole café sings 'The Internationale'.

INT. CABLES BEING DESPATCHED
FROM FRONTLINE. TRAIN

STALIN

Urgent. To Dzerzhinsky: This attack on the most important leader of world proletariat has to be answered. No mercy on agents of the bourgeoisie. We answer their terror with Red Terror. Stalin

TROTSKY

To Dzerzhinsky, Moscow. This is the second attempt on Lenin's life. Uritsky and Voldarsky have been assassinated. Two attempts to blow up my train. Response must be swift and severe.

EXT. DIFFERENT PARTS OF THE COUNTRY.

Brutal scenes. Cheka raiding offices and homes of SR members and dragging people away. Summary trials. Executions. Five thousand are executed.

INT. KREMLIN. LENIN'S APARTMENT

INESSA

Are you sure this is wise.

LENIN

I'm not suggesting you move in here, though I would like nothing better. They've found you an apartment ten minutes from here and a direct phone line. That is very wise.

INESSA

Volchik. It's so good to see you walking again.

LENIN

And I'm told you're working too hard. Not sleeping enough, not eating enough.

She embraces him, cradles his head on her breasts and neither of them speak.

INT. KREMLIN. MEETING ROOM. 1918

Politburo meeting. Huge map of Russia with Red and White positions marked. Trotsky in full military gear. Lenin in flow.

LENIN

We have received a message from Woodrow Wilson. He wants to mediate in the civil war, bring it to an end. Wants a meeting. We can't not go. Lev Davidovich, you'll have to go.

TROTSKY

A mediator? He's on the other side. He knows their gang is losing the war. I'm not going. I wasted enough time in Brest Litovsk, and all of you attacked me.

LENIN

This is different. We want nothing from Wilson. You can denounce him harshly, but you must go. Everyone agrees.

STALIN

There will be no truce. We will carry on fighting.

TROTSKY

Do we have a list of the pogroms carried out by the Whites? The number of Jews they've killed?

RADEK

Not a good idea. Wilson's an anti-Semite. It will draw him closer to the Whites. You're the epitome of the Jewish–Bolshevik conspiracy. You want to dig a deeper hole for our side.

(laughter)

TROTSKY

I am prepared to bet anyone here that the Whites will refuse. They don't want negotiations. They want weapons and soldiers and armies. I move next business.

STALIN

The Menshevik press is out of control. Lenin is a dictator, Trotsky is a bloodthirsty Napoleon, Dzerzhinsky is training executioners whose blood lust has become insatiable, and I'm a bandit, a bank-robber.

RADEK

Sounds pretty accurate to me.

(nobody laughs. Radek raises his hands in apology)

LENIN

Leave them alone. They are backing us in the civil war. Martov denounces the Whites with the same passion as Trotsky. He's intemperate. He makes us angry. The same as us in many ways. Except that we're in power.

TROTSKY

We've offered them a place in government. It's they who refuse.

LENIN

Not they. Martov. I've never known him to be so decisive in all his life. He wants to be our conscience. He doesn't want to get his hands dirty. On this he's always been consistent. Let him be.

EXT. SOME MONTHS LATER. SUMMER. STAGE IN MOSCOW SQUARE – EARLY EVENING

A huge stage. A huge crowd. Music being played. The backdrop is a set of panels by Lissitzky. The Red Wedge is getting larger and larger, and the white area is diminishing. Stage lights go up. Meyerhold's actors are choreographing the civil war.

Babel comes and whispers to Meyerhold, who is in the wings.

MEYERHOLD

Would he come?

BABEL

I can try.

MEYERHOLD

It would be fantastic. Fantastic. OK. Try.

Babel leaves. Meyerhold speaks to a leading actress who nearly faints.

A play is going on with strange gestures and disjointed, disturbing music. The audience is rapt. At the edge of the square, Babel and Trotsky are watching. Meyerhold joins them. He gives a signal to the ACTRESS.

ACTRESS

We must interrupt this play. We have news from the front. A special messenger from the train will relay it directly to you.

The audience thinks all this part of the entertainment. Suddenly spotlights target a familiar figure. Trotsky walks to the platform, is lifted on to the stage by stagehands, and speaks.

TROTSKY

Comrade Meyerhold thought I should say a few words on the situation at the front. Comrades, we are on the eve of total victory. Denikin and Kolchak are in total retreat. Within the next month, peace will return to our country and Soviet power will be consolidated. The war is over.

Applause. Shout from the audience, 'What about War Communism then?'

That too is being discussed. We are not unaware of what our people have been through ...

INT. METROPOLE HOTEL. MOSCOW.

Several hundred delegates are present. Seated on the platform, among others, are the Bolshevik leaders. Sverdlov is chairing the session. Trotsky is finishing.

TROTSKY

And thank you, comrade Martov, for only interrupting
me seven times.

*Laughter. Martov's hand has been raised for some time.
Lenin signals to Sverdlov to let him speak.*

SVERDLOV

Martov has the floor.

MARTOV

All our people are paying a heavy price for this perfidi-
ous civil war. Our party is clear on whose responsibility
it is and why the White counterrevolution has to be
defeated.

But, yes, comrades, there is a but. The methods
Lenin and Trotsky are using are unacceptable. The
taking of hostages is an outrage. Because somewhere
in a dark reactionary corner assassination plans are
being hatched. Should thousands and thousands
who have no part in these plans and are completely
ignorant of their existence ask themselves for weeks
and months on end whether this might be their last
night.

One must have a policeman's narrow mind to
believe that the threat to massacre the innocent will
deter a fanatic, a White Guard conspirator, a religious
maniac. No to these methods! The Bolshevik state
power, unaccountable as ever, during two years of
dictatorship is overgrown with a thick layer of career-
ists, speculators, new bureaucrats and plain
scoundrels.

Pandemonium in hall.

I know, I know, it's not nice when I hold up the mirror. If you have an ugly mug, don't blame the mirror.

Shouts of get him out! Etc.

Your policies are detached from the interests of the toilers. If you carry on like this, you will destroy yourselves and your beloved party. Destroy your opponents in this fashion and you will soon start killing your own. That is why you need a permanent opposition, you need elections, you need people who tell you the truth. The health of the revolution demands it.

Uproar. Lenin pale with the anger. Trotsky likewise.

                    SVERDLOV
Comrade Martov, your time is up.

                     MARTOV
What? I'm going to be executed? Now? Here? Why not? Human life has lost its value under Lenin and Trotsky.

Uproar.
  Trotsky rises to his feet in anger.
Martov stops and walks out. Trotsky follows him.

EXT. OUTSIDE METROPOLE HOTEL – DAY

Martov is coughing badly. Trotsky stops him.

                    TROTSKY
That was mean-spirited, personal ... you sound embittered.

MARTOV

You know perfectly well that if you were in my
place, you would make the same points. Power has
blinded you to reality. Lenin wouldn't, but you would.

TROTSKY

And if you were in my place, fighting a brutal civil war
in which the enemy takes no hostages and is wiping out
whole Jewish villages, how would you act?

MARTOV

I would fight to defeat them, but not in this fashion.

TROTSKY

Perhaps we should convene a special conference on
humanitarian war and kind killings.

MARTOV

Yes. Funny. But I'm warning you. Dzerzhinsky's Cheka is
becoming a collective of serial killers. They will soon
start killing Bolsheviks who disagree with their leaders
and the leaders who disagree with the General Secretary.
That is the logic that you could once see so well.

These methods – I still remember your old words –
will lead to this: the Party substitutes for the working
class, the Central Committee substitutes for the Party
and the General Secretary substitutes for the Central
Committee.

Brilliant. Prophetic.

TROTSKY

I was wrong about Lenin, but those words still apply to
the committee men.

MARTOV

They apply to you, Lev Davidovich. To you! And as if
it's not bad enough what's happening here, you want it
repeated all over the world. Splitting workers parties,
pushing, bullying your new supporters to hurry up and
make the revolution regardless of conditions. Have you
forgotten Marx completely?

TROTSKY

Everything we do is wrong, I know. How can we ever
satisfy the remnants of what is left of your faction. Were
we to blame for the disintegration of the Mensheviks,
too? Might politics not have had something to do with
it? And their craven capitulation to capitalism? Yes?
No?

Trotsky's aides come rushing to him.

AIDE

We cannot delay comrade. The train is waiting, and the
news is not good from—

MARTOV

From now on the news will never be any good.

Trotsky nods curtly to Martov and walks away.

EXT. MOSCOW. HOTEL LUX. JANUARY 1919 – DAY

*A cable is delivered to Zinoviev, who is shaken. He picks up
the phone (to Lenin).*

ZINOVIEV

It's urgent. It's Grisha. Is that you, Ilyich?
    It's very bad news from Germany. Rosa and

Liebknecht dead. Yes, I'm sure. The Embassy cabled. Of course. I'll speak to Trotsky. Fine.

Trotsky walks into his office. They look at each other in disbelief.

> TROTSKY
>
> So, it's true. You've informed Lenin?

Zinoviev nods.

> ZINOVIEV
>
> He says you should speak at the meeting tonight.

> TROTSKY
>
> This is a huge blow. It's as if we'd lost Lenin and . . .

> ZINOVIEV
>
> You.

> TROTSKY
>
> Or you in 1905.
>   This uprising was a huge mistake. The result is a catastrophe. Rosa was opposed. She thought it was an adventure. Did Radek push this or you? Where is Radek? Is he safe?

Zinoviev nods grimly.

> ZINOVIEV
>
> He'll report to the Politburo when he gets back from Berlin.

EXT. MOSCOW. STREETS.

Posters going up on walls for Rosa Luxemburg/Liebknecht Memorial.

Trotsky, Martov and friends walking past observe the spectacle silently.

INT. MOSCOW. MEETING ROOM

Lenin, Trotsky and Zinoviev deep in conversation. Huge map of the world on the wall.

                    ZINOVIEV

I'm not convinced that the German revolution is dead. It will rise again. Europe is not pacified. Factory occupations in Turin, unease in Britain . . .

                    LENIN

Possibly given the scale of the crisis. But I don't think the bourgeoisie will be surprised this time. They were well prepared for Berlin. They will make alliances with anyone and everyone against the revolution.

                    TROTSKY

We have to build a strong party in Germany. That is the key task now, but while we're waiting, we might strike the British Empire where it hurts.

                    (goes to map)

They have only 30,000 soldiers to police India. It's not impossible for us to create a special force of 50,000 from Central Asia, defeat the British and hand the country to its own people. The national movement is on the rise.

LENIN

See if it's feasible. And then there is China. Grisha, if Europe falls to counterrevolution, we might well have to shift eastwards.

ZINOVIEV

We're organising a special congress – Toilers of the East – but only after we've crushed the Whites.

TROTSKY

A year at most.

INT. APPARTMENT. KREMLIN, MOSCOW – EVENING

Inessa and Lenin.

INESSA

Did you know it would be so difficult?

LENIN

No. There are many things I didn't know. Many things we don't know. Martov, of course, knows everything.

INESSA

He's going to Germany for a conference?

He nods.

Good. For how long?

Lenin looks sheepish. He won't look at her.

Volchik. You won't let him back?

LENIN

It's for his own good. He's ill. He'll get better treatment.
Look I don't want to discuss him any further. It's you
I'm worried about. You're working too hard. It's written
on your face. You need a rest.

INESSA

I enjoy my work.

LENIN

You need a rest. I will organise a trip to the Caucasus for
you. Rest. Breathe the air.

INESSA

Only if you come with me.

LENIN

In a few years' time we might be able to do that. Not
now. So, it's settled. You will rest. The children will be
fine. I enjoy INNA's company. Nadya adores her.

INESSA

OK, OK, I'll have a holiday if it makes you happy.
And I know you'll miss Martov. I know it. However
viciously he denounces you, you fear he might be
right.

They embrace.

EXT. STREET. MOSCOW. OCTOBER 1920

*Inessa's body lies in state with women in charge. Pallbearers
arrive. Lift the coffin. Outside a funeral procession, largely
women. A coffin draped in a red flag being carried down the
street to the Kremlin. Kollontai, Nadya and others*

marching. The funeral March is being played. A forlorn Lenin, alone, has been weeping. He walks slowly.

NADYA (VO)

We never saw her again. Ilyich was devastated. Had he not sent her to recuperate, she would still have been alive. He repeated this to himself and me time and time again.

KOLLONTAI

(Whispering to Neighbouring Woman)

Look at him. I've never seen him like this. He loved her more than anything else. I hope he doesn't collapse.

The procession continues and Inessa's children are comforted by Nadya and Lenin as it reaches the cemetery below the Kremlin Wall. The three children – Inna (22), VARVARA (19) ANDRE (16) – are all hugged in turn by Lenin.
The music stops abruptly. Silence. Lenin has composed his features. Nadya is weeping.
A feminist colleague says a few words.
As the coffin is lowered Lenin whispers to Nadya. They sing 'The Internationale', which echoes through Red Square.
Lenin, Nadya, and the three children walk into the Kremlin.

NADYA (VO)

He seemed to have shrunk. I feared now for his health. He whispered he wanted to be buried next to her.

INT. MOSCOW. INESSA'S APARTMENT
– THE SAME DAY

Lenin, Nadya, Inna, Varvara and Andre in her living room. A silent tableau.

Innochka, all three of you. Nadya and I can never replace her. But for both of us you are now our children.

He bursts into tears, and Inna rushes to hug him while Nadya embraces the other two.

And we must eat together as much as we can. Andre, your chess is not up to standard. Tomorrow, 7:00 p.m. In my apartment.
I must leave you now children.

As he leaves, he strokes the piano. A snatch of a Beethoven sonata.
Kollontai and other women enter. The room fills rapidly. Drinks are served. The women sing.

INT. TENTH PARTY CONGRESS.
HALL. MOSCOW. MARCH 1921

Eight hundred delegates have assembled. Lenin walks to the platform. Applause. As he speaks the speech is illustrated with archive.

LENIN

Comrades, allow me to declare the Tenth Congress of the Russian Communist Party open.
We have passed through a very eventful year both in international and in our own internal history. In Germany, France and Italy, there are revolutionary parties that have made the Communist International part and parcel of the international working-class movement.
At home, this is the first congress that is meeting without any hostile troops, supported by the capitalists and

imperialists of the world, on the territory of the Soviet Republic.

(applause)

The Red Army's victories over the past year have enabled us to open a Party Congress in such conditions for the first time. Three and a half years of unparalleled struggle, and the last of the hostile armies has been driven from our territory – that is our achievement!

Our Party is still confronted with incredibly difficult tasks, not only in respect of the economic plan – where we have made quite a few mistakes.

Comrades, we have passed through an exceptional year, we have allowed ourselves the luxury of discussions and disputes within the Party. This was an amazing luxury for a Party shouldering unprecedented responsibilities and surrounded by mighty and powerful enemies uniting the whole capitalist world.

I should now like to deal with the Kronstadt events.

I have not yet received the latest news from Kronstadt, but I have no doubt that this mutiny, which very quickly revealed to us the familiar figures of White Guard generals, will be put down within the next few days, if not hours. There can be no doubt about this. But it is essential that we make a thorough appraisal of the political and economic lessons of this event.

What does it mean? It was an attempt to seize political power from the Bolsheviks by a motley crowd or alliance of ill-assorted elements, apparently just to the right of the Bolsheviks, or perhaps even to their 'left' – you can't really tell, so amorphous is the combination of political groupings that has tried to take power in Kronstadt.

You all know, undoubtedly, that at the same time, White Guard generals were very active over there. There is ample proof of this. A fortnight before the Kronstadt events., the Paris newspapers reported a mutiny at Kronstadt. It is quite clear that it is the work of Socialist Revolutionaries and White Guard émigrés, and at the same time the movement was reduced to a petty-bourgeois counterrevolution and petty-bourgeois anarchism.

EXT. KRONSTADT. MARCH

The fortress filmed across the ice. As we move closer the noises of people talking, slogans.

INT. KRONSTADT FORTRESS. KRONSTADT SOVIET IN SESSION. MARCH 1921

Huge banner: ALL POWER TO THE SOVIETS, NOT THE PARTIES.

PETRICHENKO

The Bolsheviks are saying we are the agents of White Guard émigrés.

(angry cries of 'Slander', 'Disgraceful', 'Show us the proof')

Let me repeat our demands so that they are clear:

1. Freedom of assembly and speech.

2. Equal rations for all working people.

3. An end to the Bolshevik monopoly of power and all power to the Soviets.

4. An end to war communism, which has wrecked the lives of peasants and workers.

I joined the fleet in 1912. By 1917 I was on the barricades. How many times did I hear Trotsky promise us what we are now asking for? Yes, it's true many of our new recruits are peasants. Everyone in Russia was a peasant at some stage, and they will be pouring into the factories too since so many workers have died in the civil war.

And how many workers have gone back to their villages because you couldn't even deliver the bread you promised us?

We are the conscience of the revolution. Don't treat us as its enemies.

INT. TENTH CONGRESS. MOSCOW.

LENIN

There has been open mutiny in Kronstadt. If the base falls, the enemy won't be able to resist the opportunity to have another go. We must crush this armed revolt.

All the delegates present, including leading comrades with experience of fighting, will have to go and help Comrade Tukhachevsky. The revolution is in danger. I especially appeal to the comrades of the Workers Opposition and other dissenting factions to join us. Comrade Trotsky is given the authority of this Congress to crush the mutiny. Time is short, comrades. The ice might begin to melt sooner than we imagine.

The whole Congress rises to applaud. Trotsky, Zinoviev and others leave the hall and head for the cars and buses taking them to trains that will transport them to Petrograd.

EXT./INT. THE NEXT TEN DAYS, 7–16 MARCH 1921

The great guns of Petrograd begin the bombardment of the island. Over the next ten days, three bloody assaults are launched against the fortress.

Red Army soldiers marching across the ice are slaughtered, but they gradually deplete the strength and supplies of the rebels.

Clad in white snow capes and bolstered by hundreds of volunteer delegates from the Tenth Party Congress then proceeding in Moscow, the troops attacked by night from three directions and forced their way into the city. Vicious fighting ensued throughout the city, and by March 18, the revolt was crushed. Scenes of executions and prisoners being taken.

Many Kronstadters, including Petrichenko, are fleeing to Finland.

NADYA (VO)

It was an ugly business. It did credit to neither side.

Most of the rebel sailors were honest young men, misled by their leaders. The Tenth Party Congress ended War Communism. We embarked on a New Economic Policy to kick-start the economy. The Congress also banned factions inside the party. Some objected, pointing out that there were no internal or external dangers threatening the revolution. Others said that it was the ultimate logic: Having expelled all other parties from the Soviet, how could you permit dissent in your own?

One night I heard Ilyich in a rage, walking up and down shouting. He was trying to convince Martov that these measures were necessary . . . but Martov's voice, I couldn't hear. It echoed only in Lenin's head.

INT. KREMLIN. LENIN'S STUDY

Lenin alone.

> LENIN
>
> I can see you with your mocking eyes. We had no
> option, Juli. If Kronstadt had fallen, Petrograd would
> have been in danger. It was world politics, not their
> demands.

> MARTOV (VO)
>
> Is there anything you can't justify? Having crucified us,
> you're now killing off dissenting voices in your own
> party. It will end badly. You're not thinking.

> LENIN
>
> Temporary measures. It's a critical moment. Remember
> what Marx wrote on the Reign of Terror? Do I need
> remind you: By its bludgeon blows the Reign of Terror
> cleansed the surface of France, as if by a miracle, of all
> the feudal ruins. With its timorous caution, the bour-
> geoisie would not have managed this task in several
> decades. Therefore, the bloody acts of the people merely
> served to level the route of the bourgeoisie.

> MARTOV (VO)
>
> He later realised it wasn't so simple. He described later
> how the revolution led to the peasantry idolising
> Bonaparte.

> LENIN
>
> We have no Bonaparte!

Give it time. That's the direction in which you're leading the party. After you die, they will fight to be Bonapartes. Trotsky or Stalin? Trotsky would be more intelligent and capable of convincing people, but Stalin controls the apparatus already.

I get all the news here in Berlin. You have some talented mediocrities on your Central Committee now, Volodya. Good committee men. They will kill what's left of your revolution. Go to bed now. You need to conserve your strength.

LENIN

I won't go to bed. You've forgotten the Jacobin disaster. How Robespierre allowed himself to be outwitted. How he was executed. Let me tell you something, Martov. That is not going to happen.

We've learnt from the mistakes of the Jacobins and the Communards. No mercy. We will show no mercy to the class enemy or even those well-meaning idiots who help our enemies. You were always wrong, Martov. Always wrong. Always wrong.

INT. EXHIBITION HALL OF THE SOCIETY OF YOUNG ARTISTS. MOSCOW, JUNE 1921

The first public exhibition of Constructivists. The artists exhibited are A. Rodchenko, K. Iogansson, K. Medunetzky, V. & G. Stenberg, A. Gan, V. Stepanova. Young people in crowd, including Inna Armand and her sister Varvara with Nadya. Mayakovsky and Meyerhold talking animatedly to Rodchenko. Babel comes up to speak with Nadya and the young women.

It's a cosmopolitan occasion as many delegates from the Third Comintern Congress are present. Nadya has had to shake many hands.

Your opinion?

NADYA

I like it. And I liked your new short story very much,
too. So did Inna.

INNA

I wept at your description of the pogrom in Odessa.

*Trotsky enters with Lunacharsky and French Comintern
delegates.*

BABEL
(Looking at Trotsky)
He knows more about pogroms in that region than me. I
will take your leave.

In another part of the exhibition.

MEYERHOLD

Strange how art blossoms as politics dies.

MAYAKOVSKY

Too cynical. As long as Lenin is alive it will be fine.

MEYERHOLD

Let's ask Lunacharsky.

*Both men go and join Trotsky and Lunacharsky. Greetings
exchanged.*

MAYAKOVSKY

Meyerhold was saying that the best impulses of the revolution are currently visible in its art.

LUNACHARSKY

Ars longa, vita brevis. Good art never dies.

TROTSKY

Talking about which, your new poem, '150 Million' is not universally popular.

MAYAKOVSKY

Oh, I know. The art for art's sake gang, led by prissy Pasternak, hate it.

LUNACHARSKY

Ilyich also prissy?

MAYAKOVSKY

Lenin hated it?

LUNACHARSKY

He sent me a message. Stupid, monstrously stupid and pretentious. Lunacharsky, I, should be flogged for futurism.

MAYAKOVSKY

But I'm a Bolshevik!
 Anyway, Lenin's literary tastes border on conservatism. Everyone knows that . . . there hasn't been a decent poet since Pushkin!

(all laugh)

TROTSKY

One mustn't empty the cupboard of bourgeois art and literature. It's necessary.

MEYERHOLD

I agree, but could not one say the same of some elements of bourgeois politics as well.

TROTSKY

No!

He walks off to greet Nadya, who is looking at a proposed sketch for a monument to the Communist International by Vesnin.

INT. SMALL HALL. AUDIENCE OF INTELLECTUALS. OCTOBER 1921 – DAY

Lenin looks extremely tired. His voice is uneven.

LENIN

You must remember that our Soviet land is impoverished after many years of trial and suffering and has no Socialist Germany, Socialist France or Socialist England as neighbours to help us with their highly developed technology and highly developed industry. Bear that in mind!

We must remember that at present all their highly developed technology and industry belong to the capitalists who are fighting us.

EXT. MOSKVA RIVER. MAY 1922 – DAY

It's raining. Trotsky is fishing. He reels in a fish and pulls it up but slips and falls on the wet grass. He's in pain. An aide shouts for help and Trotsky is helped to his car and driven home.

INT. TROTSKY'S APARTMENT. MOSCOW – DAY

Trotsky is lying on the bed resting his bandaged foot. Bukharin bursts into the room. He is horrified.

> BUKHARIN
>
> You, too, are in bed!

> TROTSKY
>
> And who besides?

> BUKHARIN
>
> Lenin is very ill. He's had a stroke. He can't walk or talk. The doctors are at a loss.

Trotsky is stunned and sits up.

> TROTSKY
>
> I damaged my foot slightly. Nothing serious. Why wasn't I informed of Lenin's collapse.

> BUKHARIN
>
> We did not want to disturb you.

> FLASHBACK

Lenin and Trotsky.

> LENIN
>
> I hope you're looking after your health.

Trotsky nods.

> Good. Otherwise the old men will die and the young ones will surrender.

INT./EXT. GORKY VILLAGE OUTSIDE MOSCOW. JULY 1922 – DAY

Lenin in normal clothes is reading documents in an armchair. Nadya and two secretaries with him. Inna and Andre kiss him before leaving. Lenin speaks and walks slowly and with difficulty.

NADYA

You can't exert yourself too much.

LENIN

That doctor thought I would never speak again. What a beautiful day. I want to sit in the garden.

He's helped by a nurse and secretaries. He rises slowly and with a stick, walks slowly into the garden and slumps into a chair. Signals his secretaries to draw closer. They sit, ready for dictation.

LENIN

This for publication in *Pravda*:
    Our state apparatus is so deplorable, not to say wretched, that we must first think very carefully how to combat its defects, bearing in mind that these defects are rooted in the past, which, although it has been over-thrown, has not yet been overcome, has not yet reached the stage of a culture that has receded into the distant past.

NADYA

Enough for today.

Secretaries return to house.

LENIN

They tell me Martov's dying, too. I told Ryazanov he
should be given everything he needs.

NADYA

If he knew it was from you, he would never accept.

LENIN

That's what Ryazanov said, but why? . . . I want to walk
a bit.

*She helps him and with difficulty he walks back into the
house. She comes out again to collect his papers and notes.*

INT./EXT. MONTAGE – DAY/NIGHT

*Lenin moving back to Moscow apartment. Attending his
office. Reading, writing, admonishing. Trotsky enters.*

NADYA (VO)

It was as if he had realised all the mistakes that needed
to be corrected, but he knew that his life would be a
short one, and he wanted to correct as much as he could.
He was especially exercised by the state of the party
itself. He asked to see Trotsky. They talked for some
time.

LENIN

Yes, our bureaucratism is something monstrous.
    I was appalled when I came back to work. You must
become a deputy. The situation is such that we must
have a radical realignment of personnel.

TROTSKY

The apparatus makes life difficult for me in the war department. Do I need to say more?

LENIN

Well, that will be your chance to shake up the apparatus.

TROTSKY

The problem is not just in the bureaucracy but the party as well. It's the combination of the two apparatuses and the mutual protection they afford each other as they surround the hierarchy of party secretaries.

LENIN

You propose then to open fire not only on the state bureaucracy, but on the Organizational Bureau of the Central Committee as well?

Trotsky bursts out laughing.

TROTSKY

I think so.

LENIN

Oh, well, if that's the case, then I offer you a bloc against bureaucracy in general and against the Organizational Bureau in particular.

TROTSKY

With a good man, it is an honour to form a good bloc.

They shake hands and smile.

EXT. FIFTH ANNIVERSARY OF REVOLUTION. BAKU. NOV. 1922 – DAY

Instructions for the Symphony of Sirens.

On the morning of the Fifth Anniversary, on 7 November, all the ships from Gocasp, Voenflat, and Uzbekcasp, including all small boats and vessels, will gather near the dock of the railway station at 7:00 a.m. All boats will receive written instructions from a group of musicians. After that, they will proceed to occupy the place assigned to them near the customs dock. The destroyer Dostoyny, *with the steam whistling machine and the small boats, will be anchored farther up, in front of the tower.*

At 9:00 a.m., the whole flotilla will be in position. All the mobile machines, local trains, battleships and repaired steam machines will arrive at the same time. The cadets from the courses of the Fourth Regiment, the students from the Azgo Conservatory, and all the professional musicians will be on the dock no later than 8:30 a.m.

At 10:00 a.m., the troops, the artillery, the machine guns, and the rest of the vehicles will also get into position, following the orders received. Aeroplanes and hydroplanes will also be ready.

No later than 10:30, those in charge of making the signals will take their positions at the regional and railway terminals.

The midday cannon has been cancelled.

The squad in charge of the fireworks will give the signal to the following vehicles for them to approach the centre with the minimum possible noise: Zykh, Bely Gorod, Bibi, Abot and Babylon.

The fifth shot will give the signal to the first and second district of the Black Quarter.

The tenth shot, to the sirens of the commercial offices, of Azneft, and of the docks.

The fifteenth shot, the districts, planes taking off, the bells. The eighteenth shot, the sirens of the square and the steam machines located there.

Simultaneously, the first company of the Military Academy will move from the square to the docks playing the march 'Varashavanka'.

All the sirens sound and end at the twenty-fifth cannon shot.

Pause.

The triple chord of the sirens will be accompanied by a 'Hurrah' from the docks.

The steam whistling machine will give the final sign.

'The Internationale' (four times). In the middle, a wind orchestra plays 'The Marseillaise' in combination with a choir of automobiles.

The whole square joins in singing on the second repetition.

At the end of the fourth verse, the cadets and the infantry return to the square where they are greeted with a 'Hurrah.'

At the end, a festive and universal choir with all the sirens and alarm signals plays for three minutes accompanied by the bells.

The signal for the end is given by the steam whistling machine.

Ceremonial march. Artillery, fleet, vehicles and machine guns receive their signals directly from the conductor on the tower. The red and white flag is used for the batteries; the blue and yellow for the sirens; a four-coloured red flag for machine guns; and a red flag for the individual interventions of boats, trains, and the automobile choir. At a signal from the battery, 'The Internationale' is repeated twice throughout the final procession. The fire of the engines will have to be stoked for as long as the signals are maintained.

INT. LENIN'S APARTMENT.
DECEMBER 1922 – NIGHT

Nadya, Inna and Varvara.

INNA

Have you heard the *Symphony of Sirens*? It was on the radio yesterday. We heard the composer being interviewed. Mama would have had a heart attack.

LENIN

Why? Which composer?

VARVARA

Avraamov. He's from Baku. He said all pianos should be burnt because they were preventing us moving forward.

All laugh.

LENIN

Lunacharsky's avant-garde is out of control. Avraamov? Avraamov? Who is this madman?
Go and play something next door while we still have pianos. I need to work.

Girls exit and his secretaries enter.

NADYA

Not too long please.

As Lenin dictates his testament, archive footage of Stalin and Trotsky.

I think that from this standpoint, the prime factors in the question of stability are such members of the CC as Stalin and Trotsky. I think relations between them make up the greater part of the danger of a split, which could be avoided, and this purpose, in my opinion, would be served, among other things, by increasing the number of CC members to fifty or one hundred.

Comrade Stalin, having become Secretary-General, has unlimited authority concentrated in his hands, and I am not sure whether he will always be capable of using that authority with sufficient caution. Comrade Trotsky, on the other hand, as his struggles against the CC on the question of the People's Commissariat for Communications has already proved, is distinguished not only by outstanding ability. He is personally perhaps the most capable man in the present CC, but he has displayed excessive self-assurance and shown excessive preoccupation with the purely administrative side of the work.

These two qualities of the two outstanding leaders of the present CC can inadvertently lead to a split, and if our Party does not take steps to avert this, the split may come unexpectedly.

I shall not give any further appraisals of the personal qualities of other members of the CC. I shall just recall that the October episode with Zinoviev and Kamenev was, of course, no accident, but neither can the blame for it be laid upon them personally, any more than non-Bolshevism can upon Trotsky.

EXT. KREMLIN COURTYARD – MORNING.

Lenin and Nadya walking very slowly in the snow.

If you really want that, you must be very concrete. No
room for doubt.

Lenin thinks and nods.

LENIN

Inessa's children. Nothing must happen to them.

NADYA

I love them, too, you know. But you've become overpro-
tective. That isn't good for them either.

LENIN

She would have been here if I hadn't . . .

NADYA

Shhh. I know. I know. It's pointless thinking about that
now. The children know how much you loved her.

He takes Nadya's gloved hand and slowly raises it to his lips.

INT. LENIN'S APARTMENT.
MOSCOW – AFTERNOON

His two secretaries are back.

LENIN

There is an additional paragraph for the testament I
dictated yesterday. I've written it down. Could you read
it back to me so that I can hear it and imagine them
reading it to the party congress.

FEMALE SECRETARY
(her voice trembling)
Stalin is too rude and this defect, although quite tolerable in our midst and in dealing among us Communists, becomes intolerable in a Secretary-General.

That is why I suggest the comrades think about a way of removing Stalin from that post and appointing another man in his stead who in all other respects differs from Comrade Stalin in having only one advantage, namely, that of being more tolerant, more loyal, more polite, and more considerate to the comrades, less capricious, etc.

This circumstance may appear to be a negligible detail. But I think that from the standpoint of safeguards against a split, and from the standpoint of what I wrote above about the relationship between Stalin and Trotsky, it is not a detail, or it is a detail which can assume decisive importance.

MALE SECRETARY
It will hit the party like a bombshell.

LENIN
Good. Type it up, let me read and sign it. So put the dates underneath where you finished yesterday and today. Everything must be accurate.

Nadya enters.

LENIN
Done.

NADYA
You know we never really knew him. He was here. We were in exile. An excellent operator, I know. But coarse,

rough, provincial. Do you remember what you said after we first saw him in London. You said this guy will cook peppery dishes.

LENIN

He's better than that, I think, but Martov, too, would use him as an example to attack us. If only Sverdlov hadn't died. The apparatus would have been healthier. The Whites said it was God's punishment for having pushed through the decision to execute the Tsar.

He suddenly falls silent and still. She's worried in case he's having another stroke. Then continues.

Some things Martov said weren't wrong. I regret we could never win him over.

Secretaries enter. Lenin signs the document and dates it. He is tired and shuts his eyes.

EXT. FLASHBACK TO COUNTRY ESTATE – DAY

A summer at Lenin's grandmother's family estate. ALEXANDER *and his brother are playing with cousins, running through the grass, diving in the river. Much laughter.*

Afterwards they rush underneath a tree. Competition to climb. Lenin does not participate. ALEXANDER *reaches the top of the tree first.*
Lenin is gazing intensely at him from below.

PRETTY FEMALE COUSIN

Look, Volodya, look! Sasha's reached the top of the tree.

YOUNG LENIN

I can't see.

EXT./INT. MOSCOW SUBURB. 1923 – DAY

Constructivist-designed workers' apartment nearing comple-
tion outside Moscow. Inside a completed apartment, the
architect is showing some workers how it works. It's one big
room. Kitchen. Bathroom. On the side what appears to be a
wooden wall.

ARCHITECT
And this can be one big room or two rooms of whatever
size you want.

He slides the wooden wall so it divides the room separating
him from the workers.

Now you have come where I am through the kitchen.
And here you can look out and see the whole play area
where the children will be playing.

WORKER
Is it really for people like us?

ARCHITECT
Of course.

INT. LENIN'S REST HOME IN
GORKY. MARCH 1923 – DAY

Lenin has had another stroke. His secretaries, nurses,
doctors, Nadya. Lenin in wheelchair points to a book on
the shelves. He is speaking in a very distorted way. The
doctor finally gets the book and hands it to Nadya. It's by
Martov.

Martov?

Lenin nods.

LENIN
Take me to Martov. Now. Now. Now.

NADYA
Martov is dead, Volodya. Martov is dead.

Lenin slumps and is motionless. Darkness.

CAPTION
LENIN *DIED SEVEN MONTHS LATER.*

EXT./INT. MOSCOW. JANUARY 1924

Archive of funeral fading into Lenin on display in mausoleum.

NADYA (VO)
I tried to stop them, but they were in no mood to listen.
Ilyich wanted to be buried near Inessa and other
comrades. He would have hated this mockery.

CAPTION
His testament was suppressed by the politburo. It was first read
out in 1956 at the twentieth party congress.

END TITLES

FINAL CAPTION
After their deaths, attempts are made to convert revolution-
aries into harmless icons, to canonize them, so to say, and to
hallow their names to a certain extent for the 'consolation'

of the oppressed classes and with the object of duping the latter, while at the same time robbing the revolutionary theory of its substance, blunting its revolutionary edge and vulgarizing it.

Lenin

Chronology of Lenin's Life and Works

1870, 10 April	Born in Simbirsk
1881, 1 March	Assassination of Tsar Alexander II by terrorist group Narodnaya Volya
1887, March	Brother, Alexander, arrested for involvement in plot to kill Tsar Alexander III
May	Alexander is executed alongside accomplices
1887–93	Lenin enters Kazan University and starts to study Marx
1895	Travels abroad: Switzerland, France, Germany
	Strikes in Petrograd. Lenin arrested alongside leaders of the Petrograd Union of Struggle for the Emancipation of the Working Class
1898, July	Lenin marries Nadya Krupskaya
1902, March	Publication of *What Is to Be Done?* in Stuttgart
1903, July	Second Congress of Russian Social Democratic Labour Party [RSDLP] starts in Brussels; Lenin elected vice-chairman. Congress moves to London

1905, 9 January	Bloody Sunday: peaceful demonstration outside Petrograd Winter Palace massacred by guards. Lenin calls for revolution
August	Tsar convokes the Duma
October	Formation of workers Soviets following arrest of railway workers' delegates. Tsar promises a new constitution to enshrine worker's rights
November	Lenin arrives in Petrograd demanding armed uprising
1906	April Fourth Congress of RSDLP in Stockholm.
July	Tsar dissolves the first Duma
1907, December	Lenin goes back into exile
1912	April Massacre of workers in Lena goldfields. Strikes across Russia. First edition of Bolshevik daily *Pravda*
1913	Lenin publishes *Critical Remarks on the National Question*
1914	In run-up to World War I, campaigns against the conflict. Socialist parties of France and Germany both vote for war credits. Brings about collapse of Second International

July	Lenin arrested in Austria after intercession from Austrian social democrats, released and forced into exile in Zurich
1916, June	Lenin finishes *Imperialism, The Highest State of Capitalism*
1917, January–February	The February Revolution
2 March	Tsar abdicates in favour of Grand Duke Mikhail; on receiving news Lenin starts preparations for return to Russia
4 March	Lenin writes 'Draft Theses'
27 March–April 3	Lenin and Krupskaya leave Berne for Zurich, and the 'sealed train' takes them back
16 April	Lenin arrives at the Finland Station, greeted by a huge crowd
4 May	Trotsky arrives in Petrograd from the US
5 May	New Coalition government formed, with Kerensky as Minister of War
3 June	First All-Russian Congress of Soviets of Workers' and Soldiers' Deputies
10 June	Large-scale demonstrations across Petrograd
20 June	Lenin voted to Central Executive of All-Russia Congress

July	Riots in the city against mobilisation turn into an improvised coup that fails. Lenin is forced into exile
7 July	Provisional government issue an arrest warrant for Lenin
July–August	Lenin in Razliv writes *The State and Revolution*
23 July	Trotsky arrested
August	Lenin is in Finland. Putsch by Commander-in-Chief Kornilov fails. The Red Army starts to grow
17 Sept	Lenin moves to Vyborg in order to be able to be involved with events in Petrograd. Party's Central Committee bar his return to the city
7 October	Lenin returns to Petrograd
9 October	Trotsky sets up Military Revolutionary Committee of Petrograd Soviets
10 October	At meeting of Central Committee, Lenin calls for armed uprising
17 October	Lenin writes 'Letter to Comrades' attacking Kamenev and Zinoviev
25 October	Lenin issues *To the Citizens of Russia*, proclaiming the overthrow of the Provisional Government

27 October	Kerensky and General Krasnov march on Petrograd and are defeated
2 November	Bolsheviks seize power in Moscow
13 November	Decree establishing Workers' control over all industries
7 December	Establishment of the Cheka, the All-Russia Extraordinary Commission for Combatting Counter-Revolution and Sabotage

1918

5 January	Lenin attends Convocation of Constituent Assembly. Bolsheviks walk out, summarily ending the Assembly
30 January	At Brest-Litovsk, Trotsky negotiates Russia's withdrawl from the war. The treaty is finally signed on 3 March
23 February	Government and Bolshevik Central committee move to Moscow
1 April	Supreme Military Council established
16 July	Tsar and family are shot in Ekaterinberg
30 August	Lenin shot by Fanny Kaplan

1919

| January | Failed coup by German Spartacists, leading to death of Luxemburg and Liebknecht |

5 February	Red Army takes Kyiv
March	First Congress of the Communist International held in Moscow
21 March	Soviet government established in Hungary
1920 January	Red Army takes Rostov
June	Start of the War with Poland
July	Red Army takes Minsk
12 October	Funeral of Inessa Armand
1921 February	Widespread strikes in Petrograd
8 March	Outbreak of Kronstadt Rebellion overthrowing Bolshevik power in the Baltic Fleet
December	Lenin told to take six weeks off by Political Bureau of the Party due to exhaustion
1922 26 May	Lenin suffers his first stroke
2 October	Returns to Moscow
5 November	Fourth Congress of the Communist International, Lenin delivers 'Five Years

	of the Russian Revolution and the Prospects of World Revolution'
23 December	Lenin suffers his second stroke
December–January	Lenin dictates his *Letter to Congress,* which calls for an increased number of members of the Central Committee and the removal of Stalin

1923

2 March	Lenin dictates his last article, 'Better Fewer, But Better'
9 March	Lenin suffers his third stroke
19 October	As his health improves, visits Moscow

1924

21 January	Lenin dies
23 January	Body is brought to London and laid in state at House of the Trade Unions
27 January	Lenin is interred in a temporary mausoleum in Red Square

Glossary of Names

Inessa Armand (1874–1920): Longtime Bolshevik feminist. Armand met Lenin in 1910 in Paris. They soon became lovers and remained close friends and comrades till her death.

Nikolai Bukharin (1888–1938): Referred to by Lenin as the 'favourite of the party', he was an intelligent economist and politician (and a very fine painter) but easily manipulated by Stalin and finally executed on his orders after a rigged trial.

Sergei Eisenstein (1888–1948): Soviet filmmaker best known for *Battleship Potemkin* (1925).

Alexander Guchkov (1862–1936): The richest plutocrat in Tsarist Russia, whose palatial mansion in St Petersburg was used as a meeting place by conservatives of every hue.

Lev Kamenev (1883–1936): 'Old Bolshevik' and longtime collaborator with Lenin. Opposed to the 1917 insurrection and, briefly, to Stalin in the mid-1920s, he was executed on Stalin's orders after a show trial.

Alexander Kerensky (1881–1970): Leader of the Socialist Revolutionaries. He was named prime minister of the Duma in July 1917 and deposed in October of that same year. His father had taught Lenin, and his son worked for the *Financial Times*.

Alexandra Kollontai (1872–1952): Early member of the Bolshevik Central Committee, and the only member to support Lenin's theses on insurrectionary strategy following the mass uprising of July 1917. She was a leading theorist on women, sexuality, the family and socialism and a pioneering organiser of the Zhenotdel.

Lavr Kornilov (1870–1918): General in the Tsar's and later the White Russian armies who briefly served as commander-in-chief in July 1917 before the 'Kornilov Affair' in August, when he was arrested for attempting a coup. Killed by a shell in battle during the civil war.

Nadya Krupskaya (1869–1939): Bolshevik activist and longtime militant, who married Lenin in 1898. She served as the Soviet government's deputy minister of education from 1929 until her death. Her Tolstoyan educational recipes often irritated her spouse.

Karl Liebknecht (1871–1919): Lifelong militant who helped launch both the Socialist Youth League and the Spartakusbund. His father was a founding member of the German Social Democratic Party. Initially sceptical of the general strike and armed insurrection launched by workers in July 1917, Liebknecht and Rosa Luxemburg belatedly joined the uprising. With no strategy in place, the insurrection was crushed within a week and its leaders assassinated.

El Lissitzky (1890–1941): Leading Constructivist artist.

Rosa Luxemburg (1871–1919): Polish revolutionary and theorist, who was one of the most creative Marxists of her time. She was murdered by the Freikorps with the support of Ebert and Gustav Noske.

Julius Martov (1873–1923): Popular leader of the Menshevik faction of the Russian Social Democratic Labour Party and close friends with Lenin. While in opposition to the party's governing right wing after the February Revolution, he also refused an alliance with the Bolsheviks. Such vacillations cemented Martov's reputation as 'the Hamlet of democratic socialism'.

Vladimir Mayakovsky (1893–1930): One of the founders of Russian futurism, Mayakovsky was a popular revolutionary poet (though not with Lenin), adored by the first post-revolutionary generation. The one poem of his Lenin praised was a savage attack on bureaucratic function and the obsession with endless meetings that resolved nothing.

Vsevolod Meyerhold (1874–1940): Leading experimental Soviet theatre director, whose emphasis on physical being, symbolism and epic theatre and whose style, philosophy and method remain a seminal influence on theatre.

Paul Miliukov (1859–1943): Principal leader and ideologue of the Russian Cadets, the nickname for the conservative Constitutional-Democrats.

Tsar Nicholas II (1868–1918): Last Tsar of Russia. He abdicated in March 1917 and was put under house arrest with his family. The Bolsheviks executed them all in July 1918 at the height of the civil war.

Georgy Plekhanov (1856–1918): Founder of the Emancipation of Labour group in 1883 and the preeminent Russian Marxist theorist from the 1880s to the 1900s. He initially sided with Lenin in the split with the Mensheviks in 1903 but soon moved to the right, becoming an outspoken supporter of Russia's participation in the World War I.

Karl Radek (1885–1939): Bolshevik journalist, who was close to both Lenin and Trotsky and known for his wit and sarcasm. Unsurprisingly, he died in a Stalinist prison.

Mikhail Tukhachevsky (1893–1937): Captured as a prisoner of war, he shared a cell with Charles de Gaulle, who could not tolerate his nihilism. After being released from prison, he returned home, joined the Bolshevik Party and became the most gifted military commander of the Red Army during the civil war. He was executed on Stalin's orders.

Woodrow Wilson (1856–1924): American president of the so-called 'progressive' era, he resegregated the federal civil service and lionised the Ku Klux Klan. This was wholly consistent with his international politics, which included sending US soldiers to Mexico, Cuba, Haiti and Nicaragua. Freud drew a scathing portrait of him.

Vera Zasulich (1849–1919): First woman to fire a revolver in Russia, she was later a member of the *Iskra* editorial board and later still a leading Menshevik.

Arthur Zimmermann (1864–1940): Senior state official in the German Foreign Office. He is best known for two acts of subterfuge during World War I: the telegram that urged the Mexican government to invade the United States and the smuggling of Lenin and other exiles into revolutionary Russia.

Grigory Zinoviev (1883–1936): Founding member of the Bolshevik Party and a leading figure in the Communist International. His show trial in 1936 – nine years after he was expelled from political leadership – was a harbinger of the terror that was to follow. He was executed on Stalin's orders.